RUSSIA

FORWARD TO THE PAST

Metro Bridge, Moscow, 2008.
Photo by Akk-Rus.

RUSSIA
Forward to the Past

Marika Pruska-Carroll

Véhicule Press

Published with the generous assistance of The Canada Council for
the Arts, the Canada Book Fund of the Department of
Canadian Heritage, and the Société de developpement des entreprises
culturelles du Québec (SODEC).

Cover design by David Drummond
Set in Adobe Minion by Simon Garamond
Printed by Marquis Book Printing Inc.

LIBRARY AND ARCHIVES CANADA CATALOGUING IN PUBLICATION

Pruska-Carroll, Marika
Russia : forward to the past / Marika Pruska-Carroll.

Includes index.
ISBN 978-1-55065-261-1

1. Russia (Federation)—History—21st century.
2. Russia (Federation)—Politics and government—21st century.
3. Putin, Vladimir Vladimirovich, 1952-.
4. Russia (Federation)—Social conditions—21st
century. I. Title.

DK510.762.P78 2009   947.086   C2009-903493-X

Published by Véhicule Press, Montréal, Québec, Canada
www.vehiculepress.com

Distribution in Canada by LitDistCo
orders@litdistco.ca

Distribution in U.S. by Independent Publishers Group
www.ipgbook.com

Printed in Canada on FSC certified paper.

In memory of my mother, Stanislawa Pruska

Contents

Preface

I HAVE BEEN SPENDING time in Russia every year for two decades. My earlier book, *Russia Between Yesterday and Tomorrow* recounted my observations of Russia in the 1990s. Now, *Russia Forward To the Past* deals with the Russian reality as it has evolved since 2000. It is based on interviews conducted between 2000 and 2007. I have spoken with Russians young and old, rich and poor, with the politically involved as well as people who shun politics, and with many who live on the fringes of society. I seek to understand Russia through the eyes of Russians, to help those in the West get beyond the stereotypes as we try to understand this complex society. To broaden the picture, I also look into history and literature, and follow the news media.

The Russian reality was difficult enough to describe and explain in Soviet days. It has become more complicated since the fall of the Soviet empire. Immediately afterward, in the 1990s, everything seemed different, new, unexpected. Russia now is even more perplexing.

My ability to speak fluent Russian is of course an advantage with regard to accessibility. In the decades that I have been chronicling Russian society I have neither asked for, nor received, any official Russian assistance.

This book concentrates on the citizens of Moscow, although other urban centres and rural Russia certainly deserve study. But one looks at Moscow first to know where Russia is heading. In the time of Imperial Russia, during the Soviet communist regime, and today, Moscow has always been in the vanguard of new trends, ideas, and developments. Whatever happens there eventually trickles down to the rest of the country. The people of Moscow are the first to change, to adapt, and to adopt. They incorporate the new and they initiate it. Listening to the opinions of a wide range of residents of the metropolis as they experience life in the crucible of developments provides us with a valuable indication of where the Russian people are heading.

Marika Pruska-Carroll
Montreal

Acknowledgments

Russia: Forward to the Past, like *Russia Between Yesterday and Tomorrow* (1995; revised 2003), is not an academic study. Instead, I have continued to observe and to communicate with Russians from all walks of life to interpret their changing realities. While in this book, unlike in the previous one, I did utilize and acknowledge outside sources, both academic and journalistic, I did not adhere to any systematic academic method in their utilization but used them to reinforce my points or to provide researched evidence to support my own personal conclusions. Therefore, the responsibility for the content of this book is entirely mine.

As always, I want to express my gratitude to all the people who shared their experiences, their views, opinions and judgments with me. I use their first names only because they preferred it this way. Those in official capacities are identified by their full names. I have made an effort to preserve my interviewees' manners of speech, to reflect their backgrounds, education, and personalities.

My gratitude goes to my friend and publisher, Simon Dardick of Véhicule Press. In more than fifteen years of our friendship and cooperation, he had always proved to be most supportive and thoroughly professional. I also wish to thank my editor Bruce Henry for his insightful comments and thoughtful editing job.

Finally, I am grateful to my students for their constant questions and unfailing curiosity about Russia. Each class taught gave me a new impetus to probe and seek the answers during my repeated trips to Russia since 2000.

Introduction

DURING THE 1990S "freedom" and "democracy" were key words in the Western analysis of Russia. To some Western observers they were an accomplished reality; to others they were tender shoots that were threatened by a totalitarianism just lurking around the corner. Russians perceived their reality differently, however. They seemed to be less enchanted with freedom and democracy because they were experiencing chaos, lawlessness, and a lack of direction. There was a longing for law and order, as the Russians understood the idea, and a genuine wish for a strong leader who would restore Russia's international status and national pride. In 2000 Vladimir Putin became just such a leader and, as some had feared in the West, he diminished democratic institutions in ways that were perceived as being authoritarian. The majority of Russians applauded Putin's regime.

Russia Between Yesterday and Tomorrow has a quotation from the independent Russian newspaper *Nezavisimaya Gazeta* that is still appropriate for the beginning of this book:

> In our blessed country, our so-called "enlightened elite" always strove toward Western models and standards. But they also succeeded in transforming these models and standards into the exact opposites of themselves. . . . Democracy in Russia looks like dictatorship and freedom looks like anarchy.

How different, then, is Russia at the end of the first decade of the twenty-first century from the Russia of the 1990s?

Moscow and a few other large Russian cities are generally twenty years ahead of the rest of the country, where not much ever changes. In Moscow a cellphone is glued to every ear. It is a city of a million of lights, as well as bars, cafés, restaurants, and casinos that did not exist only a short time ago. There are more luxury cars, and more pollution, than one could have imagined. And then there are the newly built wondrous architectural structures—the bigger the better. All of the above highlights the stark contrast between extremes of opulence and poverty. But there is also a new, growing middle class which supports a new order reinforced by propaganda via state-owned media. There is virtually no political opposition and independent political parties don't exist. The Duma, Russia's parliament, is no longer the scene of political battles, some of them physical, as it was in the 1990s. The Duma overwhelmingly supports the president and the prime minister. The majority of Russians applaud this political serenity. Once again, the country has embraced a one-party system.

In addition to the proliferation of mass youth organizations, children are mobilized into joining pro-government groups, following the familiar Soviet model. The new—or is it the old, disguised as new?—ideology is forming, and its chief slogan is "Strong Russia for Russians".

And of course there is oil. The wealth and politics of oil are making it possible for a new power base to form. They are facilitating Russia's march to a new global prominence.

How is it possible, many Westerners ask, that after nearly a century of communist totalitarianism, in a country that covers nearly one-seventh of the globe, that there might be a rebirth of dictatorship, and it might be acceptable to a majority of the population? What is it about Russia that challenges Western logic—that defies our expectations and results in the formation of a unique reality that evades labels and definitions?

To explore these questions, in addition to observing and conversing with Russians, I reviewed current literature depicting various aspects of the Russian reality and I compared their conclusions with my own findings. I am particularly interested in the subject of values related to various facets of Russian life, and how they evolve. I explored the generation gap and observed a major contrast in generational values, but to my surprise I also found that, contrary to appearances, there are more similarities than differences between the young and the old.

Undoubtedly, even with all the transformations that took place after the fall of the Soviet Union, the core of Russian society remains unchanged. It is this immutable core that links Imperial Russia with Communist Soviet Union and with today's Russia. The more Russia changes, it seems, the more it remains the same: not a new observation, but one that is reinforced by the title of this book.

Gradex Centre, Moscow.
Photo by Sergey Rod.

PART ONE

Observations and Impressions

There are about 20,000 *bomzhes* or homeless people in Moscow
Photo by Achim Hepp.

Moscow's first Apple shop, 2005.

A New Moscow — Heralding a New Russia

ANY DISCUSSION of post-Communist Russia will almost inevitably start with the capital. People say "Moscow is like a different country in relation to the rest of Russia." Moscow influences the structure of the country's economy and leads in politics, human resources, public opinion, and creative accomplishment. Moscow's influence shapes Russia's identity. According to the Russian Public Opinion Research Centre, "Anything that happens in Moscow now will follow some twenty years later in the rest of the country." It is often said that "Moscow is not Russia", in exactly the same way that Americans say "New York is not America." But Moscow has always been the trendsetter. From the best to the worst, things happen there first. It is the place to watch. From Moscow one can observe the patterns and cycles of change.

Moscow is the seat of power for the Russian Federation. At its centre is the Kremlin, the walled complex where the President lives and works, and where government facilities and embassies are located. Russia has eighty-five federal subjects (areas), two of which are cities, Moscow and St. Petersburg; Moscow being smaller in area and larger in population. Yury Luzhkov, nicknamed the "Great Builder," was the mayor of Moscow. He was appointed as acting mayor in 1992 and then elected in 1996, winning 95 per cent of the vote. He was re-elected in 1999 by 69.9 per cent, in 2003 by 75 per cent, and again in 2007. Luzhkov was dismissed by President Medvedev on September 28, 2010, after returning from a holiday in Austria, citing "loss of trust". The September 2010 dismissal followed weeks of speculation regarding Luzhkov's position, caused by his questioning of Medvedev's leadership. The present mayor is named Sergey Sobyanin and little is known about him.

Moscow is the largest city in Russia and in Europe. Its metropolitan area is one of the largest in the world. The 2002 census reported that it had 10,382,754 legal residents. For centuries it had been the largest city in Russia, and later in the Soviet Union. The collapse of the Soviet Union led to a decline in other Russian cities, so Moscow's dominance has become more pronounced. Russia has a low birth rate and a high mortality rate, and its population has been declining by about 700,000 people a year since the fall of the Soviet Union. Moscow's population, however, has steadily increased because its robust economy attracts internal migrants. To help regulate population growth, the city has a passport system that prohibits non-residents from staying for more than ninety days without registering. This was the rule under the Soviet regime and it has recently been reinstated.

Moscow is the political, economic, religious, educational, and financial centre of the country. It has the largest number of billionaires of any city in the world—seventy-four, according to *Forbes* magazine in 2007, with an average wealth of $5.9 billion each. Moscow ranks with Tokyo and London as the world's most expensive cities. It is a boom town with the prevailing attitude that people are welcome to live there as long as they can afford it. If they are not "making it", they are treated mercilessly. There is only one homeless shelter, a fifty-bed facility run by the Salvation Army. Moscow deals with the homeless by deporting them. They are dumped 50 kilometres from the city centre and warned that they will be imprisoned if they return. There are, in fact, about 20,000 homeless people in Moscow. They are called *bomzhes*, an acronym for *Biez opriedielonnego miesta zhitielstva*—outcasts without a specific address. Paradoxically, the homeless are not perceived as a major social problem. Most citizens approved of Mayor Luzhkov's deportation policy. Most *bomzhes* lost their state-subsidized apartments when privatization meant they could no longer afford them. But winners and losers—those who have found a niche in the New Russia and those who have not—do not co-exist easily in Moscow and there is little mutual respect.

Although the general level of prosperity is rising under Putin's rule, the gap in Russia between the haves and have-nots has increased enormously. Moscow is home to many of the rich, the ruling moneyed class of New Russians. Approximately seven per cent of Russia's population live in Moscow, but more than 40 per cent of its privatized enterprises are located in the city. It is an island of prosperity in an ocean of poverty. All but one of the country's top twenty-five banks have head offices in Moscow, and it is said that 80 per cent of the country's bank deposits are in Moscow banks. The banks have become richer, not by making shrewd loans, but by cultivating chummy relationships and handling transactions for the city government and the natural resource monopolies. The banks made hefty contributions to Mayor Luzhkov's pet construction projects that are found everywhere. Two examples are the Cathedral of Christ the Saviour, which has been rebuilt at a cost of $600 million, and a vast new underground shopping mall just off Red Square. These are considered minor investments by Moscow businessmen. Moscow's skyline is being remade. At street level there are colossal traffic jams and growing pollution year-round because automobile sales have increased exponentially, and it is said that half of the Russians who can afford cars live in Moscow. There is an explosion of nightlife, of prostitution, of city lights, and of up-market international boutiques. Nowhere else in Russia are so many doing as well as in Moscow.

Muscovites' personal incomes are the highest in Russia, and economists say that they are even higher than they appear because Russians routinely hide the true value of their real incomes. They are twice as likely as other urban Russians to have travelled to faraway exotic destinations. They are three times more likely to own a personal computer or a microwave and to use a credit card. Moscow has always had a higher standard of living and greater access to consumer goods than the rest of the country, but today the disparity is greater; comparable to pre-Revolutionary times when the wealth of Moscow and St. Petersburg dramatically overshadowed the rest of the country. The gap in wealth reinforces a centuries-old sense of separation in Russia between the rulers and the ruled. The fast-paced, complex world of the winners is disconnected from the world of their countrymen.

A new subject is being studied in Moscow schools: "Knowledge of Moscow". Students read fragments of literature to learn what great writers and poets have said about Moscow. They read Tolstoy, Blok, Aksionow, and Cvetaeva. They make excursions to places of importance all over the city. They study the treasures of the Kremlin and visit old neighbourhoods that still look and feel like pre-Revolutionary Moscow.

Unfortunately, more and more of the old Moscow is falling victim to mysterious fires. In 1994 alone there were suspicious fires at some twenty historical sites; causes remain unknown. They were well insured. On the presidential election day, March 13, 2004, there was a fire at the Great Manege, in Manege Square next to Red Square in central Moscow. The wooden-roofed tsar's stables, which were built in 1817 and had become the Great Exhibition Hall, burned like kindling. Problems with wiring were cited as a possible cause. But it is prime real estate.

The Great Builder Yury Luzhkov was the primary influence on Moscow's evolution. He was in his fifth term, having held office for sixteen years until he was sacked by President Dimitri Medvedev. He was genuinely popular with Moscow's citizens and its business community. He was a non-ideological Communist Party official, a bureaucrat who forged strong ties with the city's business men and women. His wife, the developer Elena Baturina, has enormous investments in real estate and is said to be the richest woman in Russia. Luzhkov supported the business community, which in turn supported him with billions that he turned into new structures including churches, parks, and monuments. He gave Moscow a facelift. The city is colourful and sleek, filled with a particularly Russian style of skyscraper and many restored fairy-tale mansions and churches. He claimed that Moscow was his only passion, and people believed him. During his tenure he was the undisputed master of Moscow's appearance, indeed, its fate, as was Stalin in the 1930s and 1940s when he ordered the destruction of part of old Moscow so he could build gigantic, twelve-lane avenues lined with office buildings, universities, and hotels in the Soviet constructivist style that appear like colossal cheesecakes on the cityscape. Luzhkov's taste was rooted in the Russian folk tradition, bizzarely combined with Disneyland.

Under Stalin about 2,000 buildings were demolished and replaced with Soviet architecture. Many were pre-Revolutionary churches. Luzhkov professed respect and affection for the past, but he was not averse to making room for new construction if the price was right. So far some 300 buildings, about forty of them considered to have had significant heritage value, have been torn down; the newest of them were built in the 1920s. The objections of heritage experts and the public have had little impact. Alexei Komech, preservationist and director of the Russian State Institute of Art History, said in a newspaper interview that he and his colleagues were ignored by the city administration, commenting that the city asked for an expert opinion, publicly acknowledged it, and then privately dismissed it. "Business considerations" prevail in decision-making, and it was Luzhkov who made the decisions.

One such demolition was the Hotel Moskva in 2004 which was replaced with a modern replica that opened in 2009. The original was designed by Stalin's favourite architect, Alexei Shchusev, and opened in 1935. It was fourteen storeys high, and notable for the different styles of its four façades. Legend has it that four design options were submitted to Stalin. He initialled the cover page as "approved" and since no one had the courage to ask him which of the four styles he preferred, they were all incorporated. The Moskva faces the northeast corner of Manege Square, steps away from Red Square. Some heritage experts were outraged at the demolition because the hotel represented 1930s Soviet vanguard architecture, while others found it an eyesore in the otherwise stunningly beautiful centre of Moscow. Every resident of Moscow who I asked about it agreed. The new hotel is operated by the Canadian Four Seasons chain.

The old Moskva was made of red and white granite. Many elite members of the Communist Party lived there, which might explain its unpopularity among Muscovites despite its 14 floors of apparent architectural merit. Shchusev was the head of Stalin's special commission charged with rebuilding Moscow in the 1920s and 1930s, and he also designed Lenin's mausoleum on Red Square. Before the Revolution he had designed churches and private residences, a talented architect whose creations reflected the preferences of the powerful. His touch has been retained in the new Moskva Hotel's façade which displays some of his designs.

The new Moscow is an amazing mélange. In the centre are massive Stalin-era constructions ornamented with socialist-realist renderings of classical themes. Small Orthodox churches scattered throughout the city provide glimpses of a more distant past. The old Arbat, a beautiful street that was once the heart of a bohemian area, has managed to preserve most of its nineteenth-century buildings. It is now one of the most popular tourist attractions. Many buildings just off the main streets of the inner city are reminders of the decadent opulence of Imperial Russia. A good number of these brightly-coloured tsarist relics have been restored and now house banks and private businesses, the only groups that can afford the location and the attendant restoration costs. Many of the restorations have been criticized, however, for compromising historical authenticity.

Real estate prices in central Moscow have gone sky-high. One square metre of space can cost US$10,000 and more. Architectural historians are outraged. Business people applaud, along with most Muscovites. Apartments at prestigious addresses that used to belong to Communist Party officials like the Kutozovsky Prospekt home of Yuri Andropov, former head of the KGB and the Com-munist Party secretary who groomed Gorbachev to be his succes-sor, are selling for up to US$10 million. Monthly rents of US$12,000 are not unusual.

Architectural historians criticize the city administration for the destruction of many historical buildings. Perhaps a third of historic Moscow has been razed in the past few years to make space for luxury apartments and hotels. Organizations such as the Moscow Architecture Preservation Society and Save Europe's Heritage are trying to draw international attention to this destruction.

Space is at a premium, so the city is building upwards. New apartments and office buildings are sixty storeys high. Many of them are right out of science fiction and they have names to match such as "Scarlet Sails" and "New Century". Other names such as "Romanov Court" reflect nostalgia for the past. The demand for apartments is so great that buildings are constructed quickly amidst controversy. Former mayor Luzhkov's wife has a near monopoly on apartment construction.

Luzhkov's aesthetic preferences reflected the prevailing popular taste of Moscow's growing middle class; he appealed to virtually every segment of the population. Citizens who cannot afford houses are grateful for every new shopping mall or supermarket. Motorists extol the virtues of Luzhkov's ugly but functional recently completed Third Circle Road, used to bypass Moscow's city centre by those who live in the suburbs. The intelligentsia were taken with his populist image and his presumed attachment to both Russia's and Moscow's heritage. He was liked by Russian and foreign business people, who were made to feel at home. Everyone was accommodated—for a price.

The only people who were not too happy with Great Builder Luzhkov's vision, President Medvedev aside, were art historians and artists who warned that Moscow was being systematically destroyed in the name of progress and modernization. Some journalists wrote about a "new Babylon" emerging at the expense of historic Moscow. They feared that Moscow was becoming a post-modern symbol of bad taste, filled with architectural kitsch and the ostentatious opulence considered typical of new money. But their voices were barely heard in the acclaim that the majority of Muscovites and foreigners expressed for Luzhkov and for the "progress" that is being experienced in Moscow.

According to a recent poll, about one Russian in five (19 per cent) want their children to live in Moscow. The second most popular choice is to have a foreign residence. Twenty-one per cent of respondents attribute the city's prosperity to the mayor; secondary factors are its status as a capital, the taxes it collects from corporations, and the abundant opportunities to earn a high salary.

Buoyed by his success, before he was ousted, Luzhkov proposed merging the city of Moscow with the surrounding Moscow Region to form a single administrative unit. The city has recently launched an international publicity campaign to improve its image abroad. There is also a new initiative to expand the city's birthrate.

We Want Cars and More Cars

LUZHKOV WAS PASSIONATE about—some would say obsessed with—transportation. It is a major issue, because the city is choking on three million and more cars every day. Atmospheric conditions are becoming catastrophic and there are a growing number of accidents. In Russia in 2007, 33,000 people were killed on the roads, about the same number as the entire European Union with three times the population and six times more cars. Luzhkov's Third Circle Road has provided some relief. It has reduced traffic congestion within the city by a factor of three or four, but experts say it will also cause more traffic fatalities. The Moscow Metro has been expanded beyond the city limits. It opened in 1935 with one line; now it has twelve lines and 176 stations. As the world's busiest metro system, it serves more than nine million passengers every day and has the longest escalators in Europe. It is also beautiful, designed to be what Stalin called the People's Palaces. The stations contain art, including murals and mosaics, and are hung with crystal chandeliers. The walls are covered in marble, malachite, and rare woods. Russians have always been proud of the Moscow Metro—it is unfailingly punctual, clean, efficient, and cheap. But it is crowded and there are long lines that extend outside the station just to get to the right platforms during rush hour. The Metro was designed to carry six million people, but its nine million daily users exceed that figure by 50 per cent. It is said that at any given time there are about two million people underground in the Metro.

Despite the new construction, transportation in Moscow remains in dire straits. In 2006 there were rumours of a proposal that only cars whose licenses end in even numbers would be able to travel on "even" days, and only those with odd numbers on the "odd" days. This was typical of the radical solutions that are always under consideration. Mayor Luzhkov was said to have favoured expansion of the bus fleet and the streetcar network. However, there are well-documented concerns that the street surfaces cannot handle the increased traffic. They are verging on collapse, literally hanging in the air over the Metro lines. More surface traffic could have tragic consequences. Since the fall of the Soviet Union in 1990 the number of cars in Russia has increased threefold while the capacity of roads has only increased 30 per cent. The worst route in Russia is the main road between Moscow and St. Petersburg, where, in 2007 alone, some 1,500 people died. The quality of the roads is poor, but the experts state that the high mortality rate is primarily related to Russians' poor driving skills and their general disregard for the rules of the road. People get away with lawless driving because of the widespread system of bribery. It is said that any ticket can be paid directly into the police officer's pocket. According to 2007 statistics, 30 per cent of drivers admit paying bribes, and 57 per cent claim that police officers forced them to pay bribes rather than receive a ticket. Another problem is the ease with which drivers' licenses can be purchased. Statistics also indicate that a quarter of accidents are alcohol-related.

Private Lives

FOR SEVENTY-THREE YEARS following the October Revolution in 1917, collective goals and objectives were of primary importance in the Soviet Union. Private, individual pursuits were at best ignored and, at worst, condemned or punished. The words "private" and "privacy" had negative, almost sinful, connotations, suggesting selfishness and a lack of adherence to communist principles. Today the right to private life is emphasized and the pursuit of private satisfaction is heavily commercialized. Without a doubt the freedom to focus on one's own well-being, rather than the good of the collective, is the most remarkable element in Russia's meta morphosis. The only limit to the pursuit of private happiness is the lack of money. Happiness is understood to be the relative ability to buy things. Without formally declaring it as an ideology, Russia has become a consumer society. The undisputed models of the good life are the lives of the New Russians. They may be admired or criticized, but they are conspicuous and celebrated. Just as the noble class of Imperial Russia set extravagant standards of lavish spending, so the New Russians epitomize the good life with their extreme display of wealth. The media frequently, in detail, extol and publicize their mansions, clothing, furs, jewelry, and other possessions. Popular novels depict their lives, magazines publish interviews illustrated with glamorous photographs, and television shows take viewers on tours of their estates. There is an obsessive fascination with the lives of the new rich. Only a handful of people question the origins of this great wealth, so quickly amassed. Any resentment is focussed on the aging remnants of the Communist Party, and is expressed during rallies commemorating May 1 or the October Revolution. Things may be changing a bit, however; the political winds from the top may have begun to blow in the direction of the oligarchs—the ostentatious display of their affluence is starting to be discouraged.

Nevertheless, extravagance and the pursuit of pleasure remain the main themes of songs, soap operas, movies, comedies, and books. "Live now, to the fullest" is the philosophy evident everywhere. Television commercials used to be translations of American advertising. No more. Western commercials never appealed to Russians, and often evoked anger and frustration. Russians don't want to hear that a product is useful or that it will save them time or money. They want assurance that they can use the product in their free time and that it will make them feel rich, or that they will be perceived as rich by others. They want to hear about style, luxury, sex, food, and easy living. They want to feel affluent, if only momentarily.

Politics rarely enters private lives. The oil is flowing, and life is better. Putin is admired. He is credited with the good life that at least some Russians are free to pursue. The bad economic news of 2008 did not have much impact on the majority of Moscow residents. The official line was that the problems were caused by the West, mostly the United States, and that Russians would weather the times with no difficulty. Some television commentators recalled that the Great Depression did not affect the Soviet Union, where it was a time of major industrialization.

How Russians Live

MUSCOVITES HAVE ALWAYS lived in apartments like most urban Europeans. Where there has never been space for single family dwellings in cities, and although there was space in Russia, there was no urban tradition of living in single-family dwellings. Dreary buildings line the streets from the centre of Moscow to its distant suburbs. This is quite distinct from the model in many North American urban centres. In Russia the dominant indicator of prestige is an address in the city core; the more central, the more posh. Factories were located in the suburbs where the less privileged, the workers, and lower-ranking employees would live. Virtually everyone lived in an apartment, although the buildings differed with respect to interior design and furnishings. The number and size of rooms, ceiling height, and kitchen and bathroom fixtures would correspond to the status of each location.

In Soviet times, apartments were assigned to people by the government. Space was allotted according to a square-metres-per-person norm. Some groups, including artists, heroes, and prominent scientists had bonus space allotments. Soviet policy was to provide basic housing for every citizen and his family. The rapid growth of Moscow's population in the Soviet era led to the construction of large, monotonous apartment blocks. They can be differentiated from each other in terms of location, age, the sturdiness of construction and materials used, or their "style". Most of these buildings were erected post-Stalin, and each style is named for the leader in power at the time of their construction— Brezhnev, Krushchev, and so forth. The buildings are usually not well-maintained; by contrast, pre-Revolutionary apartments have many rooms. The Soviet regime assigned a room per family, with shared kitchen and bathroom facilities with many others people living in the same apartment. It was very difficult for everyone. Five per cent of monthly earnings went for rent, with the possibility of additional service charges per person. Social groups congregated in their own neighbourhood, such as workers living next to the factory where they worked. There used to be a car factory close to the Avtozavodskaya Metro station. The university is near the Universitetskaya station where students and academics live nearby. There are apartment complexes for high-ranking military officers. Kutuzovsky Prospekt Street was, and remains, the location of the magnificent apartments earmarked for government and artistic elites. Some buildings are instantly identifiable by their civic address; they are recorded in the collective memory as "Brezhnev's House", for example.

Many pre-Revolutionary buildings have been renovated and restored to their earlier magnificence. The streets of "Old" (eighteenth- and nineteenth-century) Moscow, notably Old Arbat Street near the city centre, with its glorious architecture and glamorous façades, have become choice locations for the city homes of many "New Russians" whose fortunes have risen since the fall of the Soviet Union. Before 1991 most of the Old Arbat Street apartments were in disrepair. As elsewhere in Soviet days, even the Old Arbat apartments housed one family per room with shared kitchen and bathroom.

This was lower than European living standards. These families dreamed of moving into an apartment in the endless rows of buildings on the outskirts, to become the proud occupant (though not the owner, in Soviet days) of their own one- or two-bedroom apartment with a private kitchen and bathroom that did not have to be shared with other families. They would willingly sacrifice the central location for the convenience.

St. Petersburg was different. Most of the housing stock was in pre-Revolutionary style. The exteriors were charming but the interiors were in states of atrocious decay. "Modern" apartment buildings were constructed around St. Petersburg between 1940 and 1980. They were reserved for the Communist Party elite but contained few luxuries.

The situation was the same in other Russian cities, large and small. People either lived in decaying pre-Revolutionary housing with surrealistic touches of former opulence on the exterior, or they lived in gloomy, featureless, and almost equally decrepit modern apartment buildings. Miles and miles of buildings like this became symbolic of the lifestyle of Eastern Europe during the Soviet era. A catastrophic shortage of housing after World War II, coupled with a great influx of people from the country to the cities resulted in quickly- and cheaply built housing. People rarely moved because the Soviet constitution guaranteed steady employment. Many workers got their apartments through their trade unions, and they lived in them for decades. It was typical for two and even three generations to share a unit, and when adult children moved out, it would be to an apartment almost identical to the one of their parents and grandparents. The fall of the Soviet Union changed everything.

According to Mercer's Cost of Living survey based on 200 expenses related to housing, transportation, food, clothing, household goods, and entertainment, out of 143 cities on six continents Moscow was the most expensive city in the world for citizens and foreigners alike, for three years in a row (until 2008).

The process of privatization has meant that 90 per cent of Moscow's Russian residents now own their own apartments. During the 1990s it was permitted to secure property rights to the apartment you inhabited. You paid a symbolic amount, equivalent to one dollar, and assumed totally responsibility for upkeep and maintenance. For many, this has become a financial hardship because expenses exceed their subsidized rent. Water, gas, and electricity continue to be subsidized for Russians, although foreign residents must pay full price. Many elderly residents have had to move in with their children because they cannot afford their apartments. Renting their old apartments, however, provides an income. People have never before had the right to buy, sell, or rent their homes. Many of Moscow residents prior to 1991 were retired, particularly those close to the city centre. Their apartments were either inherited or purchased by younger Muscovites after their deaths.

As the free market took over in the 1990s prices and rents ballooned: the Russian and foreign business community urgently needed accommodation and office space.

With the presence of "new" money, luxurious apartments have been built in the cities, and large single-family houses were constructed around Moscow and other cities. Virtually all the pre-Revolutionary buildings in central Moscow have been restored by members of the new elites.

The middle class has taken a different course by purchasing apartments for themselves and their children, and renovating them to include modernized kitchens and bathrooms and more space. After nearly twenty years an interesting theme has emerged: anything that remotely pays homage to Imperial Russia is prized. One can enter an ordinary 1950s apartment building, walk along a nondescript corridor or ride a terrifyingly small and slow elevator, and then come to a padded double door with three locks, an alarm system, and a peephole. Inside is a revelation: the tiny entryway is lined with mirrors and crystal; the kitchen is a dream in chrome and marble, replete with gadgets and details that few North Americans would even think of, let alone be able to afford. The bathroom is more mirrors and marble, often with gold fixtures. The kitchen and bathroom are still amusingly small. The other rooms have parquet floors. Large windows with lace curtains and heavy drapes in elaborate colours and designs (a window treatment favoured throughout Europe) join walls that are usually covered in dramatic wallpaper. The appointments are usually tasteful, but more appropriate in a palace or a mansion, perhaps in another century. I have yet to see a plain wall or plain wallpaper in a Russian house or apartment. Not for Russians Scandinavian clarity and simplicity. IKEA is present, but it has adapted to Russian taste. A prominent Russian sociologist friend agreed that Russians are liable to flaunt luxuries. "It is a Russian characteristic that even the poorest people have crystalware and gold at home." He believes that the consumer boom is a compensation for earlier poverty.

A one-room apartment, thus refitted and centrally located, could easily command US$1,500 in monthly rent. Twenty years ago, it would have been occupied by an elderly widow and cost ten dollars a month; more recently, if she were still alive, she'd be living somewhere else, with her children, receiving a monthly pension of about $100.

Real estate prices are constantly rising. In 2009 on the outskirts of Moscow one could expect to pay about US$4,000 per square metre in a prestigious district. In the centre of Moscow a one-bedroom apartment would rent for about US$2,500 a month. A typical one-bedroom apartment has an area about 30 square metres (about 325 square feet), a two-bedroom is about 45 square metres (485 square feet), and a typical three-bedroom apartment is 70 square metres (750 square feet). This means that almost everyone who actually owns a Moscow apartment is a millionaire. By 2009 even the tiniest room was worth more than US$100,000. Many families could not move, especially those in the two-bedroom apartments that were granted by the state, because they would not be able to afford the rent on a new place. Some city residents coped by renting out their apartments and staying in tiny houses, *dachas*, outside the city. There have been newspaper reports of an organized crime group kidnapping Moscow flat owners to gain control of their real estate. Two suspects were arrested; they had stolen ownership of some three hundred apartments in central Moscow. In one case a man was kidnapped, falsely declared mentally ill and then hospitalized, leaving his apartment in the hands of the criminals.

Dacha

A *dacha* is a seasonal or year-round second home, located outside of the city. They are ubiquitous in Russia and some of the former Soviet republics. They are built on plots, 500 to 1,500 square metres (about one-tenth to one-third of an acre) in areas that were allotted to workers by their unions. The buildings rarely exceed 25 square metres (about 30 square yards) in size. Most of them do not have permanent heating and many do not have indoor plumbing. About 30 per cent of urban people have a dacha. There was no law banning their construction, so squatters began occupying vacant land near cities. Many were apartment-dwellers who wanted to spend time in nature and grow their own fruit and vegetables. In 1958 the government recognized their right to use the land to build a small house and to connect to the local electrical

33

and water supplies. In the 1980s the dacha boom peaked. Virtually every family with the means either had their own dacha or spent weekends with friends at their country places. Dachas provided millions of working families with an affordable summer retreat where they could garden.

With the return of private ownership, the dachas have been privatized. Russia is now the nation with the largest number of owners of second homes. Dachas became assets, reflecting the status of their owners. The better-off made dramatic improvements to their once modest dachas.

The term itself has assumed new meaning as affluent Russians build country houses worth millions of dollars. They are constructed of solid materials—brick and concrete—and they represent an elaborate display of social status, wealth, and power, featuring luxury items such as swimming pools, marble statues, fountains, tennis courts, and racing stables. Some are estates with small forests, ponds, and an airstrip for the owner's plane. Many of the oligarchs, top-name artists and entertainers, and politicians choose their dacha as their primary residence; their opulent city apartments are used only for occasional visits. Both residences have intense security—the dachas are surrounded by substantial fences topped with barbed wire, surveillance cameras and motion detectors, and in some cases, include heavily-armed guards.

This odd mix of lifestyles (city core/dacha) is not at all like North America's suburban living. Shed-like dachas and palatial dachas don't have very much in common, although they exist side by side. They do have some common denominators: the owners share poor, congested roads and long commutes. There are no schools to speak of, and certainly none that match the standards of Moscow schools. There are a few supermarkets in the vicinity, and a few health club facilities. However, the very rich are not alone in their taste for country living. Moscow's growing middle class is the largest group purchasing houses outside Moscow, although they pay the equivalent of US$1 million to $10 million at mortgage rates of 11 per cent. Often the sale or rent of their city apartment has made the dacha purchase possible.

How Russians Shop

MAYOR LUZHKOV'S VISION for new supermarkets and shopping malls apparently reflected Russians' dreams of the good life and he delivered those dreams. In July 2007 he was sworn into office extending his tenure, he thought, as mayor of Moscow to nineteen years. Prime Minister Vladimir Putin, who had originally nominated him for the mayoral post, told those present at the inauguration ceremony that Moscow had become "one of the largest, best, and most prosperous cities in Europe."

These were boom times for suppliers of building materials. Foreign producers and investors were dominant here as in many other areas. This recalled the pre-Revolutionary period, when foreign business interests dominated the Russian economy. Just prior to my last visit to Russia, the German firm Obi had opened two home and building supply stores in Moscow, each 15,000 square metres (about 160,000 square feet) in area. Several Polish construction companies were also doing well in Russia. All have had to adapt to the Russian market. Luzhkov set the tone with elaborate adaptations of the already ornate architectural style preferred by Russians. At the home supply stores people buy gilded columns, reproductions of antiques, decorative towers, balustrades, and a myriad of architectural detailing that anywhere else in the West would be considered over the top. In Russia every new single-family home incorporates "the Tsar's heritage" in façades, staircases, draperies, and furnishings. Gilding is common, and patterns are elaborate.

Luzhkov and Russian consumers were in sync with each other, as was Luzhkov and business. Grand 2 is a 140,000 square metre (1.5 million square feet) shopping and entertainment complex that has just been built near Sheremetyevo Airport by the mayor's friend Serge Zujev. It includes an enormous furniture store which only sells antique reproductions. It is said to be the largest such complex in Europe. Zujev's first mall was the extremely popular Tri Kita, which offers Moscow's avid consumers 98,000 square metres (about a million square feet) of shopping. Under construction on the banks of the Moscow River is a business centre called Moscow City. The papers brag that it will surpass its equivalent in Los Angeles.

Prior to 1991 shopping in Russia was often compared to hunting. You needed luck, skill, determination, and time to buy almost anything. The bigger the purchase, the harder it was to find. The successful completion of any buying process was celebrated. Shortages and poor quality, as well as limited purchasing power, made shopping a chore rather than a pleasurable activity, a source of entertainment, or even a passionate hobby as is so often the case in the West. In the old days, one searched for a long time for what one wanted and then waited in line, and finally endured poor, rude service. It was necessary to compromise because it was rare to find the exact item for which you were looking. Everything has dramatically changed. Just about every Western firm—from fashion boutiques to electronics giants—has an outlet here.

This didn't happen overnight. Immediately after the fall of the communist system, the streets became a marketplace. Prices changed daily, usually upward. Shopping was unpredictable and one never knew what might be available in the corner store. The state stores were almost empty of goods and customers, but they coexisted with makeshift kiosks that offered nearly everything. Competition was fierce among the street sellers—a stall might become a burnt-out shell as "market forces" competed for street corner spaces.

Street vendors have gradually been outlawed. Some stalls evolved into proper stores which co-exist with the state stores. Grocery stores were the first, but others have emerged. Ten years after the fall of the Soviet regime, the shopping patterns in cities like Moscow and St. Petersburg have changed beyond recognition. The rest of the country has followed.

Now all the stores are filled with a large selection of merchandise. Shoppers are very fashion-conscious and clothes are even trendier than in New York. Malls are springing up. Mega City is an enormous mall which opened recently about an hour's drive from the centre of Moscow. A car is necessary to get there. It looks odd to westerners; almost no customers. It is large and oddly unimaginative and prices are very expensive. I was there with a Russian who thought nothing of paying the equivalent of US$600 for a pair of Italian shoes—six months' pension income for an average retired person. In Soviet days you could generally recognize a foreigner by their footwear because Soviet-made shoes were unremarkable and uniquely shabby. Everyone aspired to own western-made shoes, especially women's shoes; they acquired fetish status. Nowhere else in the world can one see so many absurdly fashionable shoes in elaborate styles: the highest heels, the longest pointed toes, the most bizarre colours, being the most popular. The choices, like the prices, are staggering. Young Russian women are always ready to sacrifice comfort for style, and they will go to great lengths to achieve it. They outpace Europeans and they make North American women look dowdy in comparison. The Cosmo Girl is alive and well in Moscow, with the rest of the country trying hard to catch up. Considering the fact that few women own cars, their ability to get around wearing the clothes they do, especially the shoes, is astonishing. But there is a definite cut-off age as women over forty have more traditional attitudes and wear more conventional clothes.

Ten or fifteen years ago clothing from the West was admired and coveted; now it is not hard to find, although it is expensive. Malls like Mega City offer merchandise from all over the world and stores in central Moscow are even more expensive, but at least they are crowded and people are buying.

The most beautiful shopping ambiance in Moscow is found in GUM. The term is an abbreviation for the Russian for "main department store". Located on Red Square, it was built in Tsarist times in the 1890s. It successfully mixes architectural styles including Russian medieval, Victorian, and Art Nouveau. The façade is divided in horizontal tiers, faced with red Finnish granite, marble, and limestone. Each arcade is on three levels, linked by walkways of reinforced concrete. Prior to the Bolshevik Revolution it contained 1,200 stores. After the Revolution it was nationalized and continued to function as a department store until 1928 when

Stalin ordered it turned into office space. After his death in 1953, it returned to its former glory. GUM was one of the few stores in the Soviet Union that was not plagued by shortages of consumer goods. Although it was patronized by Muscovites, the lineups to purchase anything sometimes extended across Red Square. In 1991 it gradually privatized, passing through a number of owners—today it is owned by a supermarket chain. It is a popular tourist destination with about 250 boutiques featuring high-fashion brand names from the West. Locals joke that these are "price exhibitions" because so few can afford to buy the Balenciaga, Miu Miu, Lanvin and similar designer items on display—but GUM outsells Harrods of London.

A tall, beautiful Russian model I met said, "Let's not forget that money is there to be spent. If they had anything, people lost it in 1990, then again in 1993 when the Mafia took over, and again in 1998 when the market crashed. So now, when we do have money, we spend it, and the higher price, the better we like it. Spending money is sexy!" Obviously she speaks for a select group of Russians, but in Moscow her attitude is more typical than in other places.

There is a great deal of wealth in Moscow and the objects of desire continue to grow in size and price. A pair of Italian shoes no longer buys happiness. Now it takes a fancy sports car, or a personal computer with all the extras, or a marble-lined bathroom in a new single-family house. Customers flock to the Bentley showroom, where prices start at about US$320,000 for a budget model. These British-built cars have become an ubiquitous symbol for Moscow's nouveau riche with demand for the cars growing from month to month. Some customers are concerned with privacy and do not want to be recognized, so they order tinted windows. Among such owners are State Duma (parliament) deputies who do not want to display their higher than average income.

Dreams evolve in Russia, and they are increasingly more expensive to fulfill. Anything can be found, as long as you have the money to pay for it.

Bazaars and the Demographic Blues

ORDINARY PEOPLE STILL SHOP at marketplaces, most of them controlled by Azeris, citizens of Azerbaijan. The Cherkizovsky market on the outskirts of Moscow, comprised of about ten thousand merchants from former Soviet republics and China, Vietnam, Turkey, India, and elsewhere, with a daily turnover of US$30 million, was the largest in Europe. Markets were dealt a mortal blow in 2007 when Russia passed a law banning anyone but people with Russian passports from selling in a public marketplace—the result of a complex mix of politics and ideological considerations which may bring painful consequences in the future.

In Soviet days multinational traditions were vibrantly evident in the markets. Most of the traders were from parts of the Soviet empire in the Caucasus region and Asia who worked twelve- to fifteen-hour days, for precarious earnings. But the bazaars were always busy with plenty of fresh and colourful merchandise. A dramatic contrast emerged in the post-communist years. Next to Moscow's great Kiev railway station there has long been a great Central Asian bazaar where one is surrounded by the faces, fragrances, colours, and products of Central Asia. Prices were reasonable and one could always bargain. Recently the European Shopping Centre, an enormous shopping complex, was built across the street. It sells everything, but can't be compared to the bazaar—the products are packaged and you do not bargain. All mirrors and crystal, polish and sparkle, along with very high prices.

There are no Asian faces. The European Shopping Centre represented Luzhkov's vision of a new, civilized Russia. The bazaars are considered backward so they will be made to disappear with this, the prevalent vision, throughout the new Russia. In eastern cities such as Vladivostok and Khabarovsk, the markets that until recently were predominantly run by Chinese traders, are diminishing. The size and scale of their wares is decreasing and products that were once accessible to ordinary people, young and old, are harder to find.

Although there are still about six thousand bazaars in Russia, their future is bleak. For the Russian authorities it is a political decision that is related predominantly to the issue of illegal immigrants. The authorities maintain that the bazaars violated health standards; that the traders carried diseases and conditions were not hygienic. In recent years bazaars have been the scene of ethnic violence directed against Asians and people from the Caucasus region (known in Russian as "blacks"). Exploding bombs and machine-gun battles between traders and their attackers became common place, but product availability, affordability and tradition kept the bazaars busy.

However, the effects of the new law are clearly evident. The bazaars are getting smaller and inexpensive food is less available. By and large, Russians are not concerned for the ethnic traders. For the traders the only way around the ban is to acquire a Russian passport, which some are doing by marrying Russian women.

Russia's population is decreasing: in 1990 there were 150 million Russians; in 2009, 142 million. Although immigration from former Soviet republics seems to be the solution to this demographic hemorrhage, Russian nationalists are opposed and the borders are hard to cross. To slow down the population loss Russia is contemplating a new law that, starting in 2013, will allow 250,000 carefully screened immigrants to enter Russia permanently each year. Even if this comes into effect, Russians Ministry of Health and Social Affairs predicts that Russia's population in 2050 will be 130 million rather than the projected hundred million (Russian Statistical Projections, 2006), of whom 25 million will live in Moscow and St. Petersburg. Economists forecast economic problems related to demography; some suggest that 700,000 rather than 250,000 new immigrants a year should be allowed in.

These conflicting views and trends are the result of deeply felt fear in post-communist Russian society. Many people fear the threat of terrorism with a deep hostility toward Chechnya, Georgia, other parts of the Caucasus region, and Asia, a hostility which is exploited by politicians. During the recent hostile exchanges with Georgia, the Russian government removed Georgians who were illegal residents—without official permission. In Soviet days, citizens of any of the Soviet republics could travel freely in Russia without permits. But following legislation in 2007, a "hunt" took place throughout the country, focused especially on the bazaars. Illegal traders, many of them southerners, were forcibly detained and transported to police stations where their documents were examined, after which they were deported and their merchandise confiscated. Georgians and Azeris, both historically active in the bazaars, were specifically targeted. The slogan was "Russia for Russians" with newspapers publishing articles urging Russians to get involved in trading at the public markets. The results have been disastrous.

How Russians Play

AFTER DECADES OF DEPRIVATION under communism it is not surprising that Russians with money have adopted the philosophy of "live for the moment." Much has been said about the absence of a work ethic in Russia. Saving money is not popular and thrift is not admired as people spend lavishly in a long-standing tradition. The nobility in Tsarist Russia was noted for its ostentatiousness and other classes emulated the aristocrats. Today it appears that the New Russians are competing to see who can spend the most and the most quickly. This is most evident in Moscow where many behave as though their riches might be taken away tomorrow. Money has to be spent in every way imaginable. You can buy books in bars, and nightclubs sell clothes; everything is overpriced. Museums are open twenty-four hours a day as part of this sense of exhilaration and feverish drive to have fun.

There is a proliferation of nightclubs and the open use of drugs and pornography is prevalent. Like fortresses they are protected by private security forces. The decor of the clubs vary, ranging from the gilded Tsarist style to the brutal starkness of venues located in former factories.

While club hopping, one doesn't want to have to worry about driving and getting caught in traffic gridlock. Rather than using a taxi, and assuming one has the money, you opt for a luxurious government car with a siren on the roof. These cars have exclusive use of a centre lane, where they can travel at speeds of 200 kilometres (125 miles) an hour. In Soviet days these lanes were for the use of chauffeur-driven cars of high-level Communist Party officials. Now they are officially designated for those who drive for members of the Duma—traffic rules are ignored as the drivers take their customers to the club of their choice and let them out at the VIP entrance. In Moscow everyone knows that if you have to wait at the front door of a club to be admitted, you are nobody important.

Whatever defies expectations is, well, expected. Women dance on bars, sometimes stripping while they do so. Are they "working girls"? Not necessarily, but they are expensive and expect to be treated accordingly. Their handbags, denoting status—very small and costing thousands—are placed next to their owners on tiny stools that are placed there for that purpose.

Anything related to money is displayed. At the cinema, for example, one learns the production costs, and what the actors were paid. The more money involved, the more the film is worth seeing. The same is true in live theatre.

It is fashionable to buy art. A girlfriend of oligarch Roman Abramovitch is said to be buying a museum to house her art collection and he is recognized as a great patron of the arts in Russia.

After their nights of drinking and drugs, Russians who can afford it go to fancy gyms and salons specializing in biological rejuvenation. They profess great concern about their diet and health, indulging massively in botox therapy. They swear by the curative properties of the traditional Russian banyas (baths) where one may indulge in luxurious eating and drinking in a private cabin, naked, and be served by naked attendants. Men and women attend *banyas* separately. This old tradition has long been popular among all classes.

It is rare in Russia for money-making to be perceived as a self-fulfilling activity. It is popular to talk about retirement at forty. Once money is no object, the focus switches to how to fill the time. Travel is popular and the New Russians are excelling at it. Recently it has been popular to embark on two-year trips around the world. The Russian traveller is in no hurry, but she or he wishes to rest in the most luxurious setting and only the most expensive hotels are worthy of notice. The new Ritz-Carlton Hotel in Moscow sets high standards. A night in a suite can cost US$16,000. An average room costs around a thousand dollars. It is not unusual for meals to cost seven hundred dollars. But you don't have to be rich to part with your money. Even at a modest Soviet-style hotel a night's accommodation can cost around US$200.

In the Soviet days the most exclusive restaurants and coffee houses were linked to unions. Virtually every working man and woman, including people in creative professions, was a union member. The writers, journalists, architects, film, and theatre artists union sponsored clubs and restaurants where their members could gather in attractive locations with superior food at subsidized prices.

Artists, actors, writers, journalists were part of a privileged and pampered group, as long as they toed the party line. They did not have to be Communist Party members because their work served and supported the system. They carried I.D. that permitted them to meet at their clubs, cafés, and restaurants. The establishments were off-limits to anyone else, and money could not buy entrance. With the fall of the Soviet Union, things changed rapidly. The venues were no longer subsidized oases of privilege. Many were privatized and started to resemble other establishments where the only thing that counted was money. At the same time, the artists and others lost their status and buying power. A few managed to stay on top by making TV commercials. Others were left to find patrons and to compete in the marketplace. Their former haunts lost their feeling of uniqueness and their exclusive bohemian atmosphere. Young entrepreneurs are now trying to recreate that feeling in restaurants and coffee houses, in an atmosphere inspired by creativity rather than wealth, to attract people who in the past would have frequented the union establishments. Many new cafés have French names reminiscent of Paris' vie de bohème. Others, situated in the old venues, have hearkened back to nostalgic names such as The Journalists' House. Some specialize in well-stocked wine collections. Such places represent a departure from the 1990s when only opulence counted. The new establishment aims to cater to a wider clientele, reflecting the growth of the new middle class. It attracts the monied young who tend to snub the nouveau riche establishments that were so popular in the 1990s.

How to Be Safe with a Private Army

NEW WEALTH REQUIRES CONSTANT, reliable, efficient protection. Protection and security services are a growth industry in Russia. The industry grew rapidly and forcefully in the 1990s and has matured since then. Job requirements are specific: security personnel have to be young and fit and know how to use weapons, so it is not surprising that the industry employs many war veterans. Most range in age from twenty-somethings to mid-forty-year-olds, the older ones placed in the most dangerous and best-paid positions, constituting about a third of the total workforce in the industry. It is they who do most of the contract killings while the younger workers are rank-and-file enforcers and protectors.

The use of force is ever-present in Russia's economic life. Its form may change, but its presence is a given. Casual observance of laws, hazy property rights, coercion, and blackmail are part of everyday economic reality. It is not surprising that the protection business is thriving. The owners of these companies call themselves "crisis negotiators": more often than not, it is an armed negotiation.

This is all in keeping with the Russian tradition in both public and private life. I spoke with the leader of a so-called "criminal protection brigade": forty-seven, a veteran of the war in Afghanistan, and a former member of the elite Spetznaz special forces. He said, "The use of force doesn't bother me. It provides an added incentive. I like my job. I see it as our contribution to the Russian reality that today we have fewer gun battles and more legal battles.

Businessmen are finally getting the message that it doesn't pay to fool with us." When I challenged his statement he added that "there was always violence in Russia and it is not going to end any time soon. This is not Switzerland. And our services are needed because some businessmen just don't know what's good for them."

In Russia's 1990s Wild West period of rapid privatization and grabbing of national resources, there were almost daily photos on the front pages of the papers of businessmen who had been killed by competitors or former partners as truly hostile takeovers, contract killings, and shootouts were normal in Russian business. Gangsters in dark glasses and loud suits committed arson, extortion, threats, blackmail, and kidnappings, and shot business people in the hallways of their apartments as warnings. Many sought protection from these "protectors".

A solution emerged from the political life of this period. In 1993 Yeltsin introduced the new Russian Military Doctrine and the new Russian constitution was ratified. Military purges followed, especially of personnel within the Ministry of the Interior and the Special Forces Unit whose loyalty was called into question following the forced dissolution of the Duma. The most trusted, appreciated, and privileged were cast aside and whole battalions of officers became unemployed. Entrepreneurs exploited this opportunity to form private armies. The new private security structures provided protection against Mafia enforcers. New casinos, clubs, hotels, and restaurants were the first to employ professional protectors and soon virtually every business was employing these armed civilians in semi-military garb.

I was told that there had been about five million men in the Russian military and state police forces, and that during the 1990s about three million of them lost their jobs. Most became members of private armies. Many of the elite secret service and members of the best police forces lost their state jobs and joined private organizations. Young men returning from military action in Chechnya augmented their numbers. The pay was, and is, excellent.

The protection brigades have consolidated and formed near monopolies known as "private KGBs", which constitute the armies of oligarchs and lesser business people. In 1994 I witnessed an exchange of gunfire between the "army" of Vladimir Gusinsky and that of Boris Berezovsky. Gusinsky was joined by the infamous Filip Bobkov, former head of the 5th Department of the KGB, which was in charge of controlling dissent in Soviet days. Gusinsky and Berezovksy were oligarchs who controlled most of the Russian media and had become billionaires as a result of privatization. In 2009 they were on Putin's most-wanted list and lived abroad— Gusinsky in Spain and Berezovsky in England. These two former rivals are now united in being labelled as public enemies in Russia. In the West they are defended as champions of a free press. Their media holdings have been re-nationalized.

With the democratic election of Putin as president in 2000, things grew more complicated. The line between state security organs and private security has become very thin; sometimes there is no difference. Why hire a private protection unit if you can hire employees of the state as part-time protectors? Private security companies are growing closer to state security organizations so the first thing offered to a business seeking protection is facilitation of good relations with the authorities. The implications and the costs are clear to all concerned.

There are approximately 20,000 private security companies in Russia today, including about 12,000 in Moscow and St. Petersburg. They make no secret of their close ties with the Federal Security Services (the former KGB and the Military Intelligence, the GRU). According to the constitution, the only state body that can serve private interests is the Federal Protection Service, but this restriction is rarely observed.

Russia is not a safe country. It is often said that since Putin became president law and order has been gradually restored. Putin gets 85 per cent approval in every poll. But one wonders. Not long ago there were two widely publicized murders. The vice-president of the Central Bank was killed, as was journalist Anna Politkov-skaya. Others have been assassinated outside the country. Altogether eighty journalists have been murdered since the fall of the Soviet Union, and there have been countless murders of less prominent people. Such killings are perceived by private security people as problem-solving within business and politics. As Stalin used to say, "You remove a man, you remove a problem."

Contract killings are frequent, and not expensive. You can have someone eliminated at a cost ranging from US$5 to $150, the price depending on the victim's position and the circumstances. There are many people in Russia who know how to use arms, who lost any sense of the value of human life during their service in Afghanistan and Chechnya. Apparently it is Afghanistan veterans, most often former *Speznats* in their forties, who do the most expensive contract killings. The attitude is businesslike:

> Business is amoral. One has to consider pros and cons and choose the option that fits the situation best. One has to assess whether it will cost more to use the whole enforcement structure or to physically eliminate one problem.

Today, the process is reversed. In the 1990s it was privatization that was claiming most victims, but now it is re-nationalization. The methods appear to be the same.

It is said that corruption costs Russia US$200 billion a year, the equivalent of the official GNP.

Because of oil and natural gas there seems to be almost unlimited money in circulation. The prime resources were privatized, and to re-nationalize them can mean all-out war. In the last four years, Russian businesses have been plagued by raids, leading to situations where officials face off, supported on both sides by private armies. Increasingly, antagonists use legal means as well. The arrest in 2003 of Mikhail Khodorkovsky and the re-nationalization of his Yukos oil holdings is a good case in point. Lawyers involved in legal proceedings may themselves become victims of contract killers.

How Russians Die

Russians' new spending habits extend to their customs related to death and dying. It is not easy to be buried in Moscow. There are sixty-nine municipal cemeteries and five of them are very large, but they are all crowded. The cemetcry is a special place for Russians, one that plays a role in the lives of everyone regardless of age or class. Russians often visit their dead, visiting the graves not only of family members but also those of writers, artists, politicians, soldiers, and other notables. Such visits are school trips or weekend outings for the family. Everybody has favourite sites that are visited frequently.

However, to obtain a gravesite at any of Moscow's cemeteries is beyond the reach of an average person. The cost for a four metre (just under five square yards) plot is about US$75,000, a price which doubles every year. A new business has emerged: a "grave" industry with a network of "grave estate agents" who help accommodate the families of the newly dead, for a commission. The profits are greater than in the housing market.

Virtually all the municipal cemeteries have an official status of "closed" and no one can legally have anyone buried in them. It is necessary to leave the metropolitan area to find a cemetery plot. Exceptions are made, for a price: a "special offering" can reach US$200,000. Location and type of grave make a difference.

Some families spend up to US$250,000 to commission a monument by a recognized artist. Commissioned works by well-known artists mark the graves of notables. Nikita Krushchev's grave, for example, is adorned with a monument by the famous sculptor Ernst Neizvestny, even though Kruschchev had at one time publicly quarrelled with him over Neizvestny's preference for abstract art.

The demand for graves in Moscow greatly exceeds the supply. Since 1990 the average life expectancy for men has dropped from sixty-five to fifty-seven, matching that of the third world. The families of the deceased have difficulty finding graves, but for rich Muscovites it is just a matter of money.

The Kremlin Necropolis is no longer used for burials. The most prestigious burial ground is Novodevichy Cemetery in central Moscow. Boris Yeltsin, the first president of the Russian Federation, was buried there in 2007. Krushchev is there, along with Stalin's wife, the writers Anton Chekhov, Mikhail Bulgakov, and Vladimir Mayakovsky. There are scores of politicians. No doubt Mikhail Gorbachev will be buried there beside his wife, who died in 1999. A tour of Novodevichy Cemetery is a lesson in Russian history. It is probably the only cemetery where money cannot buy burial space.

The 1965 film *Doctor Zhivago* was based on Boris Pasternak's novel of the same name.

PART TWO

Stereotypes and Perceptions

Russian players, Russia-Slovakia hockey game, Vancouver, 2010.
Photo by S. Yume.

Holy Trinity Church, Ostankino district, Moscow 2010.
Photo by Lodo 27.

The Russian Soul

WE HAVE A SHORTHAND WAY of thinking about ethnicities. We say Americans are aggressive, ambitious, enterprising, always ready to start something new, friendly, optimistic, and, at times, simple. Canadians are supposedly laid-back and good at compromise, but too modest and self-effacing. The Irish are moody and inclined to drink. Germans love order and marching and sentimentality. The Poles are brave, gallant, hard-working. Brits have a stiff upper lip and love eccentricity. The French are good lovers, cooks, and shopkeepers. The Finns are gloomy, the Hungarians dashing, and the Czechs, solid. And Russians...ah, the Russians!...they have the Russian soul. They are morbid and passionate, cruel and compassionate, greedy and sacrificing, brutal yet tender...

It is hard to say how much these stereotypes reflect reality, but they are deeply rooted and persist with little change over time. It is difficult to argue against the observation that people from different nations, even different parts of one country, differ from each other. There are collective features that strengthen national stereotypes. They are influenced by national histories, cultural heritage, traditions, climate, and geography, and the difficulties of travel. At one time there was minimal influence from other cultures. But in today's global village of travel and electronic communication, there are homogenizing forces that are making people everywhere more and more alike. McDonald's golden arches are ubiquitous. Teens worldwide listen to the same music and dress and behave more or less in similar fashion.

But the process of cultural homogenization is not the entire picture. There is resistance as our need for distinctive national identities is stronger than ever and that engenders conflict.

How different, then, are Russians from people in the West? How real and far-reaching are the events of the last two decades: the fall of communist totalitarianism and the birth of freedom and democracy? What effect are these changes having on Russia's interaction with the rest of the world? How are the Russians different from others? How do we understand them, and they, us? How much do we really know about each other?

Stereotypic images are formed over time. In Tsarist Russia the external image was at one time formed from encounters with the occasional traveller, writer, opera, or business person. From this period came two stereotypes: the dashing aristocrat, and the mindless serf. The nineteenth century, particularly through the works of Tolstoy and Dostoyevsky, made the West conscious of the "Russian soul". The Soviet period produced forbidding stereotypes of Communist bureaucrats, collective farm workers, and indoctrinated robots. With the fall of the Soviet Union, new stereotypes have emerged: the vulgar new rich, the bloodthirsty mobster, the begging *babushka*. Some old stereotypes such as ruthless autocrats and an expansionist Russia are taking on new life.

What is available in English about the Soviet Union and about today's Russia presents a black-and-white picture. Innumerable paperback novels present Westerners as the good guys and the Russians as the bad. The stereotype applied in Soviet days, and it persists. There was a period in the 1990s when authors of popular novels were confused about who the villains were. But now, as during the Cold War, the Russians are back—even when they are not bad, they are different and not to be trusted.

But some interesting literary works provide vivid, authentic, and telling pictures of Russians and how they perceive Westerners: not always flattering, but they avoid stereotyping and provide some insight into the Russian mind.

> The Russians are a mass of contradictions. Capable of all sorts of excess. When they are joyous, it is one endless banquet. When they are sad, it is a massive state of depression. When they are angry it is a tantrum. Everything is excess. Love. Hate. Suspicion. When it comes to suspicion, they are absolutely beyond comprehension. They think of themselves a healthy body about to be besieged by a pack of enemy viruses. Even when they are happy there is sadness in their joy. (W. Adler, *Trans-Siberian Express*)

The young German writer Ingo Schulze paints a darker picture.

Russia—all you can do is leave it. All week I have been wondering why I was doing it to myself, why I was in this city and not in Paris or Italy. It was as if the people here only recently came in from the village and don't know how to walk down the street. They plod along, yelling, shoving, elbowing, and spitting. No one says "excuse me." They pay no attention or just bellow swear words. And everywhere, like some peculiarity of the climate, is this stench of old farmer's cheese, embedded filth, and cigarette smoke. Sometimes there is a little gasoline in it, or garlic, or toilet bowls. From courtyard doors drift odds and ends of meals, stairwells reek of piss. And when it comes to people, you don't know if they have taken on the stink of their surroundings or if it is coming from them. (*33 Moments of Happiness: St. Petersburg Stories.* Knopf, 1998)

Writer Colin Thurbon travelled to Siberia and wrote about the rarely seen new Russia.

The air in parks clattered with pop music. Clusters of mini-skirted girls paraded their irregular beauty and children strolled with their parents in sleepy obedience; but their jeans and T-shirts were stamped with stars and stripes or Donald Duck. Every other pair of shoes or trousers sported a pirated Western logo. Fast-food restaurants had arrived, a rash of small shops and a kiosk had appeared, selling the same things. Yet, a feeling of boredom, or of waiting, pervaded the city. All style and music, the new paths to paradise, seemed synthetic, borrowed. Real life remained on hold. . . . A pervasive frustration proved that freedom, once again, had proved illusory. Scarce jobs and high prices were the new slave masters. (*In Siberia,* Harper Collins, 1999)

Thurbon visited Omsk, a medium-sized city some 500 hundred kilometers east of the Ural Mountains. The Trans-Siberian railway line passes through it. Russians there told him:

> As Moscow appears to sink deeper into the embrace of the West, so Siberia becomes enshrined in the Slavic imagination as the Russia that was lost, the citadel of the spirit. The mystique of a chaste, self-reliant Siberia rises again. Siberia is more Russian than Russia is, people say, as if it were a quintessential Russia, or the imagined country which Russia would like to be.

And a Siberian priest from Irkutsk, a city at the base of Lake Baikal, said about America, "America is godless. Nothing good can come from there. Only videos and that music, nakedness, AIDS, everything. America will not help us."

The Five Days War in Georgia in 2008, as depicted by Western media, affected the perception of Russia in a dramatic fashion. The West has had little good to say about Russia. There was a constant talk about the "worsening pattern of behaviour" and it was repeatedly stated that Russia was in danger of damaging its international reputation. A new survey commissioned by Britain's *Financial Times* indicated that Europeans consider Russia a greater threat to global security than Iran, Iraq, or North Korea. These sentiments are echoed in North America.

I wanted to find out what "ordinary" people in the West know, or don't know, about Russia, and what their counterparts in Russia think about the West so I talked with Western business people, students, journalists, and tourists about their perceptions of Russians. I interviewed Russians about their experiences with the West and Westerners.

How We See Russians

I ASKED MY STUDENTS in Montreal what they thought of Russia, surveying about five hundred students over a five-year period (2003-2008), including students who were starting a course on Russian politics, and others who were taking unrelated courses I was teaching. This inquiry extended to friends and acquaintances, using an eight-point questionnaire, with written answers which I organized by topic and ranked in frequency of recurring key words and ideas. The students' responses were compared with those of others. They followed similar patterns, although there was variation depending on the respondent's education and depth of knowledge. Canadians and Americans were included in the survey. There were few differences in the responses, although Canadians tended to see hockey and climate as two things that Russians and Canadians have in common, and Americans did not make such observations. Americans tended to see Russians as people who subordinate themselves to authority for the "collective good", and they noted that Russians have been subject to continuous cruelty due to war, police oppression, and other institutionalized causes.

When I travel to Russia each year I also visit other Western European countries. In 2003 I conceived the idea of doing this book and have since taken the same questionnaire with me, interviewing about fifty people, friends and strangers, in England, Germany, Poland, and Holland. Without exception, they are better informed about Russia than North Americans. I will return to them and their responses later on.

The eight points and a summary discussion of responses follows.

1. What is the first thing that comes to your mind when you think about Russia?

People were asked for three words, names, or ideas. The overwhelming majority said, "Communism" as their foremost association with Russia. It was the first choice for 90 per cent of the respondents. The second most common association was "vodka" and its excessive use, at 70 per cent. The concept of vastness was a close third—Russia's huge land mass. About 50 per cent of respondents thought of poverty, although people weren't sure whether individual Russians were poor, or the whole country. Fifty per cent of respondents mentioned the tsars and knew they were unelected absolute rulers, but didn't really know whether to compare the tsar to a monarch, president or prime minister. Students were generally aware that a revolution had occurred in Russia near the beginning of the last century, and that the last tsar and his family were executed. Forty per cent of respondents associated Russia with the Cold War. Respondents unanimously considered Russia the bad guy in the Cold War, although the reasons for that, other than a vague sense of "they were Com-munists", were not generally understood.

Twenty per cent of respondents named the following ten items. First was literature, although few could name any Russian writers except for Tolstoy, Dostoyevsky, and Gogol. Architecture was next, although the only examples were the onion domes of Russian churches and the red walls of the Kremlin. Stalin, Gorbachev, Yeltsin—the three names came up with the same frequency. Also mentioned were nuclear war, Siberia, snow, and the KGB. Siberia was believed to be a place of labour camps and political persecution. All of Russia was thought to be cold and snowy. For many people, Russia and Siberia were almost interchangeable. The KGB was invariably considered dangerous and sinister and continuously spying on the West.

Ten per cent of responses listed eighteen things, names, and ideas: revolution, Gulag, Bolshevik, Mafia, chaos, endurance, disintegration, pollution, Moscow, waste, repression, military, Chernobyl, Chechnya, Peter the Great, figure skating, classical music, and caviar. Almost all the respondents knew of Putin, but few knew the term "New Russians".

2. Do you know any Russians?
Only a few answered in the affirmative. Most of the students had never met a Russian. The twenty who had actually met one or more Russians, had come into contact with a diverse lot. It included a hockey player, a high-school exchange student, a beauti-

ful Russian met in Paris, and a descendant of an aristocratic Russian family. One student had worked as a bellboy in a hotel in Cyprus and had come in contact with hundreds of rich New Russians who spent plenty of money on vacation. That was, in fact, why he had decided to take my course on Russia. Some people had met some Russian immigrants. One student was of Russian origin. One had visited Russia. The general rarity of encounters with Russians means that the answers to the next question were mostly based on preconceived notions and stereotypes.

3. What are Russians men/women like?

The answers to this question are particularly revealing. The images of both men and women were derived from two contrasting sources. One was American visual stereotyping in films, newscasts, and even advertising and the other was Russian literature. Most of the images were more influenced by the former.

Respondents influenced by American media described Russian women as stocky and overweight. They were described as badly dressed housewives, burly babushkas in kerchiefs regardless of their age, masculine-looking. In terms of their social standing, character, and personality, Russian women were perceived as overworked, always tired, traditional, prematurely old, and male-dominated, and as having very little to say in public life. Nevertheless, they were also seen as hard-working, resourceful, and compassionate. A good number of respondents saw them as bossy, gruff, and even abusive. There was an obvious contradiction in these perceptions, but the respondents seemed unaware of it. Respondents who indicated familiarity with Russian literature, or at least with movies based on Russian literature, were more likely to think of Russian women as romantic, sentimental, strong, determined, fatalistic, spiritual, self-sacrificing, often mystical, and very sexy. There was no such disparity in the perception of Russian men. They were uniformly seen as big, bulky, strong, heavy, badly dressed, loud, cigarette-smoking, vodka-drinking, and often drunk. Russian men were perceived as cold, unemotional, rigid, tough, insensitive, bossy, sexist, narrow-minded, very traditional, and conservative. Only a few respondents found more positive words to describe Russian men. These terms included hardworking, very intelligent, creative, used to hardship, hospitable and ready to share, idealistic, spiritual, frustrated fatalists, cultured, amiable, and proud. Both men and women were seen as patriotic people with a strong sense of values who lead sad, miserable lives.

4. What Russian movies, or movies about Russia, have you seen? What Russian books and authors can you name?

I asked these questions to find out the sources of my respondents' ideas about Russians. The primary source of images and ideas was Hollywood movies. In order of popularity, these included *From Russia with Love*, *Crimson Tide*, *The Hunt for Red October*, *Reds*, *The Russians are Coming, The Russians are Coming*, *White Nights*, *The Russia House*, *The Inner Circle*, *Gorky Park*, and *Moscow on the Hudson*.

The writers named were Dostoyevsky, Tolstoy, Gogol, Pasternak, Pushkin, and Solzhenitsyn, in that order. Among the novels identified were *Crime and Punishment*, *The Idiot*, *War and Peace*, *Anna Karenina*, and *Doctor Zhivago*. A few respondents knew of Nabokov's *Lolita* in print or movie version.

The overall impression of Russians that people took away from these movies is negative. With few exceptions, the Russians characters come across as controlling, domineering, threatening, dangerous, and untrustworthy enemies. The Americans and other Westerners are portrayed as trustworthy and altruistic. However, in literature Russians were found to be sensitive, truth-seeking, long-suffering, and giving.

5. Can you identify a newsworthy moment that relates to Russia?

Most people mentioned the breakup of the Soviet Union, but few remembered the date. Some took notice of the Chernobyl nuclear accident of 1986. Others thought of the Berlin Wall coming down in 1989. A majority of respondents thought that anything related to Gorbachev, Yeltsin, or Putin was newsworthy. Interestingly, the names Gorbachev and Yeltsin evoked a positive response, while Putin did the opposite. Chechnya was identified as a name in the news, but few respondents had any idea why.

6. What do you consider the most interesting thing about Russia?
Surprisingly or not, most people thought of Russian culture, although they were not able to be more specific than that. In second place were sports, with hockey named most often. Achievements in space ranked third, although people were aware that Russia's achievements in space were in the past. The mysterious "Russian soul" ranked fourth, considered something unique to Russia but not easily understood; many thought it had something to do with excessive drinking and some kind of spiritual values, while others thought it had to do with the experience of hardship. In fifth place was ballet, an art in which Russians are perceived to be particularly gifted.

7. Does anything about Russia frighten you?
Virtually every respondent named the nuclear arsenal as Russia's most frightening aspect . Its technical ability to destroy the world was the foremost thing on people's minds. Nearly all were also concerned about the possibility of nuclear accidents in both the military and electricity-generating spheres. The second concern, expressed by half of respondents, was that chaos and anarchy could emerge in Russia. They were concerned about political instability, the threat of a return to communism, and the danger of growing fascism. Even in this context, the nuclear threat is primordial; people worry that the means of mass destruction may fall into the hands of criminals or unbalanced individuals. About 25 per cent of respondents were afraid that changes in Russia may lead to a new Cold War.

8. Can the Russians be trusted?
I was surprised to learn that half of respondents felt that Russians can be trusted. Many qualified their answers by saying that while the Russian people can and should be trusted, their political leaders should not. Others felt that there is no choice: if

the West and Russia are to co-exist, they have to trust each other. Others said that Russia doesn't follow reason in its actions and therefore should never be trusted. The most moderate advocates of distrust stated that it was "too soon to trust Russia."

Western European respondents were more descriptive in their answers, rarely answering with just a word or a name; almost everyone came up with an idea.

"Before I went to university," said a young Englishman, "I saw the Russians as enemies. Then I saw them as victims, and now I don't know how to view them."

"It is one of the biggest countries in the world, and it is one of the most oppressive and undemocratic," said a Dutchman.

A German respondent said, "It is at a crossroads. It may go forward or it may go backward."

"It is oppressed by politics, all the time," said another German.

"It is a beautiful, miserable country," said an Englishwoman.

"When I think of Russia, I think of poverty and a lack of freedom," commented an elderly Dutchman.

"I think of vastness and cold," said a German woman.

"I keep thinking about food lines and shabby-looking people," said an English cab driver.

But another Englishman mentioned some very wealthy Russians he had encountered as a waiter.

"For me, the first thing that comes to mind is Red Square and marching people. I saw it so many times on the telly," said an older saleslady in London.

"I think of red flags, communism, and labour camps," said a middle-aged German.

"Russia is the land of my ancestors," said a young German student. "It is a country that has produced great works of art and has great culture, despite the odds."

"I think of drunk, depressed, and oppressed people," said a middle-aged pedestrian in Amsterdam.

A number of Dutch students who had recently visited Russia, however, talked about how expensive and decadent they found life in Moscow.

"It is a great country, and a dangerous country," said another German.

I was surprised at how few people knew any Russians personally. The younger the respondent, the more likely they were to have met Russians. Sometimes it was by serving wealthy Russians who were visiting their countries as tourists. Some young people I surveyed had visited Russia, between 1995 and 2005. Generally speaking, the Western European perception of Russia is vastly different from the North American. The most frequent response was, "Russians are like people everywhere." Western Europeans now think of Russian women as belonging to one of two species: older *babushkas*, and beautiful, exotic, and even wild young women.

The West that New Russia Loves to Hate

IN THE MID-1990S, the New Russia was lashing out at the West and at the United States in particular. There was a growing sense among Russians, reinforced by the media, that the country had been relegated to the periphery of American interests. "Now that we are no longer considered a threat, Americans feel they can push us around," was a frequently expressed view.

The situation with NATO was touchy. The inclusion of a number of Eastern European countries in NATO was perceived by the Russians as an insult and a threat. The NATO bombing of Bosnian Serbs and NATO's presence in Kosovo did nothing to lessen those feelings. A second point of conflict was the issue of conventional-force reduction. Russia's position was that the West should not expect it to honour the treaty signed in 1990 restricting Russia's freedom to station tanks near its borders. Russian generals believed that since the Soviet Union and the Warsaw Pact no longer existed, the treaty had lost its validity.

Private and official voices in Russia were expressing the deeply felt sentiment that Western offers to support Russian democracy were not sincere. Russians perceived that the West was playing games and could not be sincere in its expressions of friendship for Russia, while at the same time the West was reassuring the former Soviet satellites that it would protect them against Russia.

Galina Sidorova was a political advisor to Andrei Kosyrev, the former Russian foreign minister. She was quoted in a Russian newspaper in 1994:

> The West's reservations toward Russia are generally based on an unspoken sense of Russia's supposed pecu-liarity as a nation with an allegedly eternal incompatibility with the surrounding world. Is partnership possible in such a situation? If the West based its strategy on a presumption of Russia's guilt and concern about her size, geography, and future sins, then our fragile partnership risks remaining in an embryonic state.

Many people felt this way.

Throughout the 1990s there was a conviction among ordinary men and women in Russia that the West wanted Russia to be weak, and to exploit this weakness.

After the turmoil of the 1990s, a radical shift developed in Russia's political reality and public opinion. Putin's Russia began to assert itself economically and politically to the acclaim of the Russian people. The new reality had an enormous impact on Russia's self-image. A sense of humiliation and weakness that had been present in the 1990s was being replaced by growing pride and an accelerated longing to "restore Russia's greatness".

The Five-Day War with Georgia in mid-2008 had a tremendous impact on Russian self-esteem. It created a negative impression in the West, but Russians applauded it as Russia's return to the international scene—that Russia had re-asserted herself as the key political player in the Caucasus region and that she had sent the West a clear message that it would not tolerate interference from the West or NATO in the "near abroad", as the former Soviet republics are now referred to.

Anti-Western attitudes intensified as Western criticism mounted. Radio Liberty interviewed Russians following the war.

They expressed overwhelming support for the Russian military action, and great hostility to the reaction of the West. "I think Russia's actions were absolutely correct," one Muscovite said. "They showed that we could be strong and that we could be right, righteous, and just."

"It's time for Russia to get up off its knees," another Moscow resident said. "We should be able to stand up for our own interests by now. One should be patriotic. Our country may have its shortcomings, but many things are not the way they ought to be. One should always be proud of one's country."

Recent polls demonstrate that public support for the Russian government is higher than at any time since the collapse of the Soviet Union. At the same time, Russians' views of the outside world, especially the United States, are at new lows. The Levada Centre (the Russian National Public Research Centre) has found that 67 per cent of Russians have a negative opinion of the United States and 39 per cent a negative impression of Western Europe. These proportions were reflected in my conversations and interviews with individual Russian friends and acquaintances.

"America and NATO have been goading Russia for years, yet they have been bombing countries right, left, and centre for the last ten years!"

"Stop reading and listening to brainwashed Western news. The West is to blame, because they are greedy and get rich from wars. The Georgia war was started by Georgia and funded by U.S. interests."

A Quick Look at Recent History
Russian attitudes toward Western Europeans and North Americans were formed over a long period. Westerners are always aware of differences when Russia meets with the West.

Peter the Great was known for his directness and lack of pomposity. In 1716 and 1717, the Tsar visited the Netherlands and France. During his visit to France he shocked the French royal court by giving Louis XV, then seven years old, what became a famous piggyback ride. This is perhaps not surprising when one recalls that they were were relatives of the monarchs of Europe, and felt most at home in their courts.

Meetings between Russia and the West took on a new character under Stalin, Krushchev, Brezhnev, and Yeltsin. These leaders represented a different civilization. The largely unacknowledged differences between Russia and the West led to crises.

In February 1943 at the Teheran Conference, Stalin used gestures that were characteristic of a Russian demonstrating friendship. He was generous in his accommodation of Roosevelt's agenda. He declared that the Soviet Union would enter the war with Japan two or three months after the war in Europe was finished. He toasted the United States and Great Britain. His every move was carefully planned and calculated, but the actual details of the discussion were barely touched on by the Soviets. It was Churchill, not Stalin, who suggested a percentage of influence that the Soviets would have in the Eastern European countries. Stalin barely glanced at the map and nodded. He kept his word scrupulously, however, and stayed away from Greece. He cared, but it is not the Russian style for the top person to appear to be concerned with details. The leader's job is to create the right atmosphere and make symbolic gestures.

Krushchev didn't behave any differently. He looked into Eisenhower's eyes, fulfilling the spirit of Geneva. He decreased the size of the Soviet Army. All Western attempts to understand and explain his motives ended in failure. Soviet actions had to be accepted as a given. No rationalizations could be found. When he tried to place atomic warheads near North America without prior warning, precipitating the Cuban crisis, the West acted in shocked disbelief. It did not occur to Krushchev to compare his action with the placement of American missiles on bases in Turkey, although that could have established a rational basis for negotiations. Kennedy, following his own Western logic, quietly removed the rockets from Turkey.

The battle between the Soviet style of symbolic gestures versus the Western style of calculated, carefully planned moves continued during the Brezhnev era. Brezhnev always gave dignitaries souvenirs. During an impromptu evening visit, as witnessed by Henry Kissinger, he personally delivered gifts for all the members of

Nixon's family. The gesture led to a tearful and heartfelt offer to solve the issue of China. During American political visits in the Soviet Union to supposedly resolve global political problems, there were trips to Crimean caves, toasts, and the giving of presents, a notable absence of political discussion, analysis, or argument. Such topics were, if anything, avoided. The negotiations carried on by teams of specialists from both sides would have come to nothing if the Soviet leader had not felt that the atmosphere was "just right".

According to American foreign policy analyst Strobe Talbott the state of Soviet-American negotiations is logical at every step. The Western mind abhors chaos. In everything, it seeks a classic battle of arguments, culminating in a sensible compromise. Not so for the Russian mind. For Russians there is always a conflict between the heart and the brain, between feelings and reason, and between symbol and analysis. For the brain to deliver, the heart has to feel right.

Gorbachev, although he was acclaimed for his "new thinking" and his "Western ways", was not really much different from his predecessors. He too needed, and used, symbolic gestures. The day before his monumental decision regarding the reunification of Germany, he took the visiting Chancellor Kohl on a tour of his home town, Stavropol. He and Kohl walked up and down streets that were dear to Gorbachev's heart. He flew Kohl by helicopter to a tiny cottage in the nearby mountains and spent the evening telling the chancellor about his childhood. Did they discuss the future of the world? The Warsaw Pact? NATO? No. For Gorbachev it was more important that they establish a personal link, give and receive moral credit, and look each other in the eye.

It is probably painful for Russians to admit, but these gestures, so important for them, have been of no significance for the West. Political historians have a reserved surprise and a certain sense of discomfort about Gorbachev and Shevardnadze's haste and their emotional impulsiveness. The time Gorbachev and the American president spent fishing in Wyoming, the exchange of gifts, passionate speeches following many toasts, these moments of crucial decisiveness to Russians, are not even mentioned by Western commentators.

Yeltsin's erratic behavior sometimes embarrassed Western leaders. There was a feeling that he needed to be contained. He never really lost the reputation of being a loose cannon.

Putin, however, is short on gestures. He is popular among his countrymen, but style-wise he is the least Russian of leaders. He does not appear to care whether he is liked, and he insists on being respected and feared. Only President George W. Bush "looked into his eyes and saw his soul." Few others have been able to accomplish this.

A Matter of Business

The reliance upon symbolic gestures is also evident in Russian-Western business relations. A Western businessperson who wants to conclude a business deal arms himself with lawyers, data, knowledge of the law, and a computer. He or she wants a detailed discussion of all the fine points, all the pros and cons, and the legal and regulatory context. The Westerner wants to eliminate the element of surprise. He expects to compromise: in every deal you give and take. The Russian businessperson coming to the West or preparing to meet Westerners in Russia has a different approach. He takes with him the most attractive, though not necessarily the most efficient, secretary and a fat chequebook. Edward Topol, in *Red Snow* (Penguin, 1984), has written, "The Russians just couldn't understand business without vodka and women."

The Russian spends a few days with his potential business partner, doing his best to make the meeting as informal as possible. When he finally decides that he has established the appropriate personal ties—that translates for the Russian as emotional contact—trust has been established. Once this has been achieved, the deal is on. The handshake is sufficient. The details and the relevant laws are not so important for the Russian. Contracts are often signed without being read.

In Russia, even basic production relations are much more heavily influenced by personal contact than they are, for instance, in the United States. The efficacy of any regulation depends to a large degree on which bureaucrat is applying it and to whom it is being applied. Paradoxically, Russian bureaucrats are on average far more flexible than their counterparts in most Western countries. An American officer will usually adhere strictly to the letter of the law, whatever the circumstances. If the law or regulations allow something, the officer will allow it. If not, forget it. A Russian bureaucrat, by contrast, is prone to feel his emotions. You can get his sympathy by crying, or his support by threatening him. (Vladimir Kvint, *The Barefoot Shoemaker: Capitalizing on the New Russia*, Arcade Publishing, 1993)

Here we have an intercultural crisis. The elements of the deal that are crucial to the Western businessperson—analysis, compromise, clear understanding of obligations and responsibilities— do not seem to matter to the Russian side at all. The Russian treasures the emotional ties that he or she believes have been formed, the tuning in to each other, the look of things, the intensity of activities indulged in together, the sharing of moments. These determine whether it is going to be a good deal or not. If a Russian does not like you, he will not do business with you, even if it might have been in his best interests to do so.

Russians are generally very secretive, and with foreigners even more so. The foreigner's nationality is unimportant; all that matters is that he or she is not Russian. That doesn't mean a stranger on a train won't tell you his life story, particularly if he senses that you are not interested.

The potential for conflict is evident from the beginning, with, on the one hand, the desire for analysis and close scrutiny, and, on the other, an emotionalism and need for a feeling of loyalty. In early stages, these two foci may interact, but it soon becomes apparent that they have altogether different priorities. What is important for one side is irrelevant for the other. Bitterness and resentment can result; embarrassment follows; irritation and mutual accusations may not be far behind. Often the deal does not get off the ground, or it may fall short of both sides' expectations. Real problems are created by mutual misconceptions and by an ignorance of each other's habits and cultural differences, and as Kvint states "Cut off so long from the rest of the world, Russians have an inferiority-superiority complex about foreigners and an idealized image of Westerners."

Even if these perceptions are not entirely accurate, they persist. Particularly prevalent is the image of the American with his feet on the table. Russians find this boorish and offensive. Kvint goes on to say that "Americans often find Russians terribly and unnecessarily formal. This is not without some basis, although Russian formality is only skin deep, like American informality."

I have had numerous experiences with students from Russia. Unlike North Americans, Russians dress up for exams. They are puzzled about the manner of dress of Western students, especially in circumstances that they feel call for greater formality.

I have no doubt that these perceptions will change somewhat, and that they are already changing, because young Russians seem different from former generations, even if those differences are only superficial. Externals are changing beyond belief, and young people are active in the New Russia, but it remains to be seen whether the inner depths of Russia will change as a result, or whether Russia's traditional political culture will once again prevail and dominate every sphere of life.

PART THREE

Generation Gap—or Not?

Umka (Anya Gerasimova) singing at the Deserted Hills festival, an open air music event held near Tarusa, Russia. June 2006.
Photo by Alexander Konovalenko.

Russia Between Yesterday and Tomorrow Revisited

IN HISTORY A DECADE is a very short time, but for a country undergoing a dramatic transition it can be both a short and a long time. Russia began a period of major transformation at the beginning of the 1990s. The changes were most profound during the early years of the decade and, I was fortunate to chronicle some of those moments in *Russia Between Yesterday and Tomorrow*. The second half of the decade was a time of repetition or reinforcement of trends, moves, moods, tendencies. On the eve of the new millennium, Russia, with its tendency for the dramatic, took a sharp turn. Literally. On New Year's Eve 1999 President Yeltsin resigned his post. Putin's ascendancy as his successor marked the new millennium in Russian life.

I watch Russia closely. As I visit familiar places, see old friends, and meet new ones, I find patterns repeating themselves, except for one major difference: now there are fewer older people and more young ones. It's a sad fact that the life expectancy for Russian men in 1995 was fifty-seven, meaning that ten years later an entire generation of middle-aged men with whom I met is now gone. But the key social, political, cultural, and economic concerns continue to evoke the dominant questions of the 1990s that were never resolved. The central question remains: what is the right way for Russia? It burns with the same intensity now as it did a decade ago. There have been years of disillusionment, disappointments, frustration, apathy, and cynicism, but a new generation repeats the same question that their parents and older siblings asked. They probe the issues of the free market and democracy, freedom and its limits, values and their meanings, nationalism and globalization. The questions are familiar, but the young people seem different from earlier generations. They are no longer in awe of the West because they are quite familiar with it. They no longer apologize for the past, since they don't perceive themselves as its makers. They are quite willing to embrace some of the old

73

Imperial and Communist symbols if they believe that they suit their Russia.

Many features from Russia in 1990 are recognizable today. There is the search for new, uniquely Russian paths. Also, there are concerns about the limits on freedom of expression, alongside a puzzling degree of apparent acceptance of Putin's measures to ensure law and order. Whether these measures relate to terrorism or to taxes matters very little. Just over ten years ago the West sounded the alarm about the danger of a return to totalitarianism, and now the alarm is sounding again. I believe, as I did ten years ago, that it is an oversimplification of a far more complex situation. I consider myself fortunate to have been there at the beginning of Russia's present transformation and to be able to continue observing its changing destiny.

Russian Youth and the Generation Gap

THE MOOD BETWEEN generations is increasingly confrontational. Throughout Western Europe people say that the age bomb is ticking. People argue that a flood of pensioners is washing away the foundation of the state, that growing armies of the elderly are straining public institutions.

Stereotypes change slowly, but it is glaringly obvious that there is a gap between older and younger Russians. Projections are that by 2030 every third Russian will be *stariki*—part of the over-fifty generation—and each pensioner will be supported by two working people. But the Russian population is also shrinking—there are eight million fewer Russians today than there were in 1990.

Increasingly heated verbal duels take place between the generations as traditional respect for the elderly is being replaced by the cult of youth imported from the West. Not so long ago, the older generation dictated lifestyle, choice of profession, and even choice of partner. The only way a young person could gain prestige and authority was to get older. Today it is the older people who are being pushed to the margins of society.

Only a few years ago it would have been unthinkable for a young person to remain sitting when an older person stood on the bus or metro. Today it is much more likely that one older person will stand up for another. One sees this everywhere. Young people, at best, don't notice their elders, or, at worst, insult and abuse them. Life experience and wisdom do not count for much in a marketplace where knowledge becomes dated more rapidly than clothes. To listen to the young, their sense is that the older people never really knew anything very useful anyway and, besides, it is the old ones who were responsible for installing, supporting, defending, and deforming communism in the former Soviet Union, or capitalism in the West.

In Russia the generations over thirty refer to the younger ones as "play-kids" whose motto is "Let's play. Let's go faster." It may appear odd to include people in their thirties in the older generation, but it is accurate since they are part of the establishment in the eyes of the twenty-somethings and teenagers because they are slowing the game by holding jobs the young ones want and exercising a caution that the young detest. But it is this middle generation, referred to elsewhere in the world as the "sandwich generation", which carries the heaviest social and economic burden. They have responsibility for the elderly and they have to care for the young, who often detest them. The generation of people between thirty and fifty-five feel trapped. The older they are, the more they resemble their elders in behaviour and attitudes. The situation is quite different from in the West where pensioners and baby boomers are relatively wealthy, healthy, and powerful. Most of their Russian counterparts are poor, sick, dying, and defeated, although they are still numerous and they make a difference at election time. Unlike young people, they vote, and they have strong political views. They are ready and willing to exercise their civic rights and responsibilities so their political convictions will have a dramatic impact in the not-too-distant political future around the world. The younger generation is concerned that the net result will be a demographic dominance. They believe that their relationship with the older generations is becoming more strained as time passes.

But observers can be easily deceived by appearances: with each passing year the underlying values and convictions of young Russians, regardless of age, are not as far apart as they may appear. The young echo the beliefs of earlier generations, parallel in many ways to those of their parents and grandparents.

What Happened to the '90s Youngsters?

IT IS INTERESTING to take another look at the group of young people I observed in the 1990s. On the eve of the year 2000, they were between eighteen and twenty-nine and ten years later some were entering middle age. Statistics are telling about the group born between 1968 and 1980, whose lives and values were shaped by the period of stagnation under Leonid Brezhnev, perestroika under Mikhail Gorbachev, and all the radical changes that have occurred since the collapse of communism. Twenty-five million Russians came of age in the period when the Soviet Union dissolved, Communist Party rule ended, and the state planning system was dismantled.

I managed to contact some of my earlier subjects. They and their friends and acquaintances seem to be doing well financially and professionally. All have cars, TVs, cellphones, computers, and most own a house or apartment; more than half, however, are divorced.

Their average income is two or three times what their parents make. Most speak English, travel abroad, and, overall, are satisfied with their lives. But they all complain about the corruption, poor health care, and deterioration of public services. They are not enthusiastic about any of the Soviet-era leaders, and believe that Lenin and Stalin did harm to Russia and the Soviet Union. In contrast to their parents' generation, they are extremely critical of Brezhnev. Nor do they praise Gorbachev or Yeltsin. Unlike their parents, but like the generation younger than they are, this group likes Putin. Unexpectedly, they also like the last tsar of Russia, Nicholas II.

They cherish family life, even though they don't seem to be very successful at making their own families, and they think friends are extremely important. Money is equally important, and satisfying work is also high on the list of priorities. More than half of them claim to be religious, although they do not all attend religious services. They tend to romanticize Russia's past, like historical movies and nineteenth-century novels. The younger they are, the more likely they are to extend their romantic vision to the Bolshevik Revolution and the Civil War.

They are disgusted with America as a collective image, and with '90s-style capitalism. They say they detest the New Russians, even though some of them can be categorized as such. They support law-and-order oriented political platforms but the older they are the more likely that they shun organized politics. They all want Russia to be strong and respected. Putin's general appeal relates to their perception that "he is bringing Russia back from the abyss of chaos and lawlessness."

"We Are Cosmopolitan Citizens of the World"

YOUNG RUSSIANS and other Eastern Europeans are in love with globalization. Participation in the processes and institutions of democracy is of less interest than participation in the global economy. Information about Western protests against multinationals, the World Bank, or the International Monetary Fund is received with astonishment and incomprehension. For young Russians and Eastern Europeans, globalization means an always available passport and the freedom to travel anytime, anywhere, with laptop and Internet access. It means the freedom to get any CD or book, foreign goods in stores, CNN and MTV. These realities are ones against which the young in Russia and its former republics and satellites are not going to protest.

Part of their image of the good life comes from the West. Possessions are very important, and they believe that the ability to purchase things is a measure of achievement. However, the youngest "capitalists", those in their twenties, have a wider claim than their immediate predecessors, those in their thirties and forties. The older group is chiefly consumers, but the younger ones see themselves as not only consumers but also investors and "cosmopolitan citizens of the world". The earlier generation's infatuation with everything Western during the Soviet period has changed into something more complex and critical. Young people no longer wish to simply emulate. They want to feel, participate in, and contribute to global culture. The distinction between "Western" and "global" is no longer clear. I spoke with many young musicians and artists who firmly believe that their artistic creations are more important and of greater significance to Russian youth than cultural products coming from outside of the country. More and more of the young "consumers" of the arts share this view. The fascination with, and enthusiasm for, the West that characterized the 1990s has been replaced with skepticism and even a degree of hostility. These feelings are being exploited by the Kremlin as part of the process of constructing a new Russian identity.

How Much Is It?

It seems clear that today's youth have different priorities and loyalties than previous generations. In the not so distant past, the priorities and loyalties of the young were shaped by the Communist Party. Today it is more complicated. Marketing executives compete with the state for the pocketbooks and minds of Russian youth. Western and Russian businesses are fighting intensely for market share and solidifying loyalty to their products. It makes sense to mold the young into tomorrow's devoted consumers, since the sixteen to twenty-five age group constitutes over 35 per cent of Russia's population of 142 million. This cohort seems to be particularly interested in Western products and brands and grew up surrounded by Western-style consumerism, some-thing which is foreign, even revolting, to their parents and grandparents. Russian youth are behaving in a manner indistinguishable from their Western counterparts: they are eager to try brand-name products; they have money to spend, possibly even more than their peers in the West. Russia still subsidizes a large portion of housing, health, and education expenses, leaving many with proportionally more discretionary income for luxuries. Russian young people are more likely to live with their parents, who provide the basics, than Western youth.

A typical young Russian, as defined in a national market survey, is twenty-four, single, living with his or her parents, and earning about US$800 a month. The parents, who are often university-educated, earn about US$400. This group of "typical" young Russian consumers is small, about six per cent of the population: a total of nine million people. They live in the city, usually Moscow or St. Petersburg. They will, obviously, have a great impact on Russia's future. This group spends about 80 per cent of their income on discretionary items. While they differ from their age peers in the rural areas and towns, the difference is less than the ones between the generations. Young people everywhere in Russia are economically more independent than ever before.

The Western companies with the highest visibility in Russia today deal in fast-moving snack products such as soft drinks and pizza, Coca-Cola, Pepsi, Sprite, 7-Up, Pizza Hut, McDonalds, as well as Mars Bars, Snickers, and hundreds of others. Alcoholic beverages and cigarette advertising is ubiquitous. Everything is permitted, including the distribution of free samples of alcoholic drinks and cigarettes during advertising campaigns. As in the West, the companies try to associate their products with fun, sponsoring events and organizing special promotions, the most popular among Russian youth involve sports and music. Some TV commercials are identical to Western ones, and others are made specifically for the Russian market. MTV-inspired advertising is proving just as popular in Russia as elsewhere. Pepsi's international campaign with the Spice Girls, which of course was not made for Russia, turned out to be immensely successful there.

Professionally-run dance clubs (the Russians still use the term "disco") are mushrooming in the major cities and throughout the regions. They are also the major venue for product promotion. Sprite, produced by Coca-Cola, has a near-monopoly among teenagers, affiliating itself with fashions and magazines that are popular with youth who frequent disco-clubs where free CDs of Sprite's jingle and dance music is distributed freely. Sprite's main rival, 7-Up, owned by the Dr. Pepper/Snapple Group, focuses on another craze—in-line skating, sponsoring a roller-blade competition in Moscow several years ago that has since become a tradition. Pepsi capitalizes on Russians' love of soccer as a corporate sponsor of the new Russian soccer league, targeting a slightly older segment of young people.

Promotional giveaways work very well for cigarette companies. Russia represents a huge opportunity for tobacco companies which are losing revenue in the West, since Russians have always been heavy smokers. Smoking is a common denominator that unites the generations. Older Russians still smoke a lot despite the potential for harm, and increasingly young people are taking up smoking. Along with attractive young women distributing free cigarettes at music and sporting events, the companies advertise on billboards and print their logos on sports clothes and accessories purchased by the young. The most successful brands are Marlboro, Pall Mall, and Camel, and smoking them is perceived by the young as cool and sophisticated.

To be cool one must also have a cellphone. Russians of all ages are obsessed with mobile phones. This is understandable, because in Soviet days and even today, many Russian homes did not have a private phone. It was a luxury, primarily because of the lack of a communications infrastructure. People used public phones, which were plentiful and nearly free of charge—a penny per phone call. The telephone system was heavily subsidized by the central government and, of course, totally controlled. Today it appears that every Russian has at least two cellphones. Like Western teens, young Russians everywhere feel that one cannot be without a cellphone. They are not cheap, and most parents cannot afford to pay for their kids' phones, so Russian teens have to earn their own money to get this "must-have" item. Their cellphone is the barometer of their social life and their social status. Rich kids have the latest models paid for by their parents. The ultimate status symbol among Moscow teens is the iPhone. Ordinary kids have an ordinary *oneo*—often second-hand—and poor kids are out of luck. Cellphones are often stolen, never to be recovered.

Although as consumers the young are different from the older generation, it is only a veneer because, paradoxically, the young, with all their global preferences, think of themselves as Russians first, and long for the world to "respect Russia."

We Are Connected

THERE IS MORE THAN one Russia. There are the people living in large cities, and then there is the rest of the country. Moscow and St. Petersburg, the largest cities, have between them 25 million people, nearly 20 per cent of Russia's population. The differences between people living in the large cities, particularly these two, and those living in Russia's many towns and villages, is staggering. A twenty-year time lag is evident in every area of life, but it is most apparent with respect to computer literacy.

According to a survey by Internet Monitor, reported in July 2008 in *Kommersant Daily*, one of Russia's most influential papers, Russian Internet users are more highly educated than European surfers, with 69 per cent of Russian users having higher education compared to 48 per cent of other Europeans. Russian surfers are more likely to have travelled abroad and have a higher income. On average, the Russian user goes online for 49 minutes per session and most of them began using the Internet in the last two years. In the summer of 2009 there were eighteen personal computer users for every thousand Russians. (In the United States there were 565 per thousand.) The Russians' numbers were to double within the year. The report saved the most revealing fact for the end: 80 per cent of all PC users live in Moscow or St. Petersburg.

There are numerous paradoxes, however. There are still few computers in the countryside or small towns. In many places where they are accessible to the public, they are barely used. Nizhnyi Novgorod is a medium-size town in central Russia, population about a quarter million. There, I witnessed bank tellers doing calculations on a computer and then checking the results on an abacus. The abacus is very much in evidence in banks, stores, post offices, and other establishments, even in Moscow. Outside Moscow and St. Petersburg, computers are viewed as creatures from another planet.

To the computer literacy gap one can add the generation gap. Few Russians over forty, even in the two biggest cities, are at ease with computers. The younger they are, the more likely they are to use computers. If they don't own one, they probably use one in the private school their parents are paying for, or in the Internet cafés that are springing up. These youngsters, as a rule, know English or another Western language and use computers with the same ease as their peer group in North America or Western Europe. Young residents of St. Petersburg and Moscow are generally sophisticated computer users, but being young increases the likelihood even if one is not affluent or a resident of either city.

As is often pointed out, one of Russia's main assets is its highly-educated population. Massive popular exposure to computer technology didn't begin until the mid-1980s during Gorbachev's perestroika. In the post-communist Russia of the 1990s, however, education was no longer provided by the state on the same scale. During the twilight of the Soviet Union, only a select group of the young political, scientific, and military elite became immersed in computer culture. President Putin, now in his mid-fifties, belongs to this group. He and a small group of other men and women have computer skills that match their western counterparts.

This led to a rather amusing international incident. In the first year of his presidency, he met with his fellow leaders at the Group of Eight summit in Japan. He suggested that they all communicate by e-mail, but the proposal ran into a snag. It turned out that he was the only head of government of the Group of Eight who knew how to use a computer. Some did not know the difference between a mouse and a keyboard.

Putin's familiarity with computers is not typical for Russians of his generation. At the beginning of the century, only 2.2 million

Russians were using the Internet. In 2008, this figure had risen to 20 million, 15 per cent of the population. Online retailing is set to "explode", according to investment counselors Brunswick Warburg. The e-revolution may have as great an effect on Russia as the Bolshevik Revolution did. In the summer of 2009, only four per cent of Russian households were equipped with a personal computer, compared with 28 per cent of Western European households. Because land phone lines in Russia are of poor quality and scarce, mobile phone sales are rising faster than computer sales, and they are becoming the primary Internet access point for many Russians. Credit cards, nearly non-existent in 2000, were in evidence in every city in the summer of 2009. The cost of personal computers and of Internet access has fallen dramatically. The number of house-holds with computers was expected to double within the next year. According to Russian Internet Monitoring IV, in 2007 15.4 million Russians over eighteen were using the Internet. The average age of Internet users was thirty-one. A further 28 million received information from the Internet via friends or other direct users.

The educational system has changed in the past decade. People are now saying, "You get what you pay for," and the most affluent parents in Moscow and St. Petersburg are sending their children to private schools where they learn not only computer skills, but also foreign languages and business skills. Virtually all of these children have their own computers.

A great disparity has arisen within the Russian education system where there had always been great respect for traditional learning. Throughout the Soviet Union school was free and text-books and curricula were standard. Now, state elementary and high schools are still free, but the best teachers are in private schools, which have entirely different curricula. They are accessible only to the few, and are located in Moscow and St. Petersburg—the great divide is in place and growing all the time. Today in Russia there is a reversal of the Soviet past—a sound universal education has been replaced by high-quality education for the elite and an inferior education for the majority. It is already apparent that the profile of Russian society is changing. The large, older, highly-educated population is wasting their still considerable potential, and losing their skills—especially Russian scientists. They are losing touch with their disciplines, and have a sense of being devalued and under-appreciated. Meanwhile, younger Russians can no longer take for granted that they will receive the standard high quality education of their parents and grandparents.

Nonetheless, the computer is reaching everywhere. Colin Thubron (*In Siberia*, Harper Collins, 2006) recounts an encounter in the city of Khabarovsk (population 600,000) near the Chinese border, about 300 miles (about 480 km) north of Vladivostok. There, Thubron met a woman who told him about her daughter. "My daughter is twenty," she said. "Do you know what she did? She went somewhere in Khabarovsk and bought herself an e-mail connection. So now she gets information from abroad! E-mail! When I was twenty, I barely dared to buy a stamp. But she and her friends see things differently."

I also met a number of young people living outside the two large cities who are connected to the Internet, and if they are not, have access to Wi-Fi at their local coffee house. They were connecting with the global village in a way their parents could not have even imagined. This fact alone has greater implications for the future than almost anything else.

Children of Privilege

I was talking with Natasha, a Moscow teenager. We met in a crowded downtown bar called Quasar, a popular after-school teen hangout, and a destination when you skip school. Most of the patrons were high school seniors. The bar was dingy, smelled bad, and was full of cigarette smoke. On the walls posters advertised Western beer and soft drinks. The techno music was deafening. I was the only face over thirty. Natasha and her friends sat on bar stools or wandered around smoking, showing off their six-inch plus platform shoes, their bell-bottoms, or their skinny pants and skinny tops, and drinking the occasional beer, Coke, or 7-Up. Natasha is slim and tall with the mandatory long straight streaked blond hair. She looked very much the same as every girl in the place. When anyone new came in—no adults of course—there would be a shocked double-take when they saw me until Natasha reassured her friends, "It's okay. She's from Canada." Her parents are friends of mine. I hoped to meet some of the teens later in a quieter spot. I succeeded in interesting a group of twelve of them to meet me in a park where I recorded two hours of impassioned conversation.

Meanwhile, I tried to look cool perched on my bar stool. I noted how little this crowd differed from their counterparts in Western Europe or North America. They have adopted every minute detail. Loud music, wacky shoes, retro clothing, nail polish ranging from yellow to the very popular black, and long straight hair for girls, while shaved heads were favoured by the boys. They all watched American movies and were crazy about American movie idols. They talked about drugs and sex, and either indulged in both, or wished they did. Computer games were very much part of the scene. For the equivalent of a few dollars you could use the computers at Quasar. Or you could play laser tag for the equivalent of US$10.

Ten dollars is a lot of money in a country where pensioners have to survive on pensions of US$120. I was curious where they got their money, knowing that so many families try to get by on as little as US$300 a month. I asked around. It turned out that these kids are mostly children of the rich, and accessing money is not a major concern.

Quasar was owned by a British man. Many of the bars and restaurants in Moscow have Western owners. They make a good profit catering to the young Muscovite generation of consumers who want Western culture, now. A young clientele that cannot get enough of Western movies and especially music and MTV. Unfortunately, they are also at high risk of drug addiction as well as STDs and AIDS.

These are the teens that are targeted by Western advertising. They are still subject to its influence—they buy it—but I find them far more sophisticated than teenagers I met a decade earlier. Like the twenty-somethings, they exhibit more skepticism and caution when bombarded by ads. They have developed a healthy distance from advertising, where a decade ago their counterparts embraced it totally and without reservation. Both teens and those in their twenties prefer Western products, and they share the belief with the New Russians that the price of the product correlates to its value. Bargain hunting is not for Russians. If you buy it cheap, it must be worthless. A well-known anecdote illustrates this:

> Two Russians meet on the street. One says to the other, "That's a great leather jacket you're wearing! How much did you pay?" "Two hundred dollars" is the answer. "Where did you get it?" "In a boutique on Arbat Street." "You fool! You could get the same jacket for five hundred in a boutique on Manezhna Street!"

Paying more for things is synonymous with higher status. Kids will brag about how much they paid for something, upping the actual price. To impress your friends, you try to buy a more expensive brand, and you want this brand to be clearly visible.

Still, it must be understood that the kids who frequent Quasar, at the time of my visit in 2009 one of the city's most popular hangouts, did not represent the majority of Moscow's or Russia's teenagers. They were the most visible, however, and they were quite defensive about that. One of Natasha's friends told me they see themselves as the "bravest". Natasha's crowd, I would find out later, was not interested in politics. They had no experience of the Communist past. It was not even a memory. Born in the 1990s, they did not associate deprivation with communism. That has made them radically different from their older siblings. They didn't have associations that people in their twenties did. I believe it was a factor of their age, and their naïve faith in miracles that will evaporate as they enter their twenties. Also, this select Moscow in-crowd was quite different from their counterparts elsewhere in Russia; they were not a typical group. They were visible primarily because of their parents' financial standing. Their lack of interest in anything remotely political was scorned by other teens as well those in their twenties and thirties. When I talked to Misha, a young business executive in his thirties, he told me he could not relate to the kids under twenty at all. It seemed odd to hear this from him, because he was a marketing professional, responsible for targeting teenagers in commercials for jeans.

"My generation was 'against'," he told me. "We knew we were against the communist regime when we were teenagers. These kids don't reject anything. They grab anything and everything. Western clothes, movies, music, culture—they want it all, without any discrimination or distinction. They eat it up! They are consumers, and that's all they are." To my surprise I found out later on that Misha's judgment was a great over-simplification. Things are not always what they seem to be.

Little Teddy Bears, *Nashi,* Young Guards, and Marching Together

I URGED MY RESPONDENTS to speak with me about patriotism, nationalism, political parties, and political participation, inviting them to comment on public festivities, demonstrations, and displays. We talked about flags and other national and political symbols and rituals. I asked them about their feelings about wars, military and civic duty, and how they envision their political responsibilities.

Virtually everyone in their teens and early twenties said that "big politics" is boring. When I probed to find out what "big politics" meant, the uniform response was that it had to do with foreign policy, geopolitics.

"I love Putin," said another Misha, a seventeen-year-old Moscow high school student. He was one of nine kids who had gathered to speak with me. They all readily agreed that they "love Putin." "He is a good president," said eighteen-year-old Alya, and others nodded. They have friends who belong to Nashi ("Our Own"), a pro-Kremlin youth movement. On March 3, 2008, some 5,500 young people connected to Nashi marched on the American embassy to celebrate the election of Deputy Prime Minister Dmitry Medvedev as president, and to protest American foreign policy and alleged interference in Russian internal affairs. With the city's blessing, thousands of pro-Kremlin young people marched across central Moscow and created some of the worst traffic jams ever seen in the city. But the key attraction of being part of Nashi, or having friends who are, is the perception that it is "right".

"Why do you think it is right to belong to Nashi?" I asked.

Dima thinks that it is pointing the way for the future of Russia. Since it was a view that I heard echoed by a majority of my young contacts, I probed further. "Russia always needs a father figure, and Putin has become Russia's father," says Dima. Dima is perceived by the rest of the group as a leader, and is its most vocal member. "We had Ivan the Terrible, we had Peter the Great, we had Josef Stalin." Others nodded in agreement. Acceptance and even admiration for these acknowledged totalitarian leaders appears to be universal. These young people are keen about the need for law and order which they see Putin effectively promoting.

Adulation of Putin crosses all generational lines. Nearly 90 per cent of Russians rank him highly. With those numbers, he may be the world's most popular political leader. There are Putin-inspired books, T-shirts, and calendars. There is also a hit song, known to all the teens I spoke with: "I Want Someone like Putin" is sung by the very popular Russian girl band Singing Together.

This was my first group of high school-age respondents, and I was curious to find out if the views they were expressing were held by other young people. I discovered that there was a direct correlation between their level of affluence and the political views they held. The better off interviewees, the ones attending the more affluent schools and whose parents had more money, were more likely to be enthralled by Putin and Nashi. That applied more to the high school group than to those in their early twenties or older. Also, their political enthusiasm was far more influenced by their friends than by any genuine interest in politics or any real knowledge of the political process with its parties and the evolving issues. When I spoke with teens from more humble backgrounds I heard a different reality. Vanja is the seventeen-year-old son of a woman I interviewed for my earlier book about Russia in the nineties. He was only three when I met his mother and father. They are working-class people living in one of the sixties-style apartment building known as Krushchevki, buildings constructed during the Krushchev era (1956-1964) and noted for their poor quality, in a neighbourhood of similar apartments in Moscow's Avtozavodskaja region, named after a metro station. It surrounds an automobile factory, which provided employment to most of the people living there. Vanja's mother was a clerk in the factory and was now unemployed, and his father was an assembly line worker there. Now fifty, he was also laid off and was working with another man fixing "anything mechanical" as he put it. They were poor, but they are a bit better off now than they were in the nineties, and they have been very supportive of Putin.

I asked Vanja to gather as many of his friends as possible and meet with me in a local park. Through him, on three occasions I met with fifteen boys and girls who all live in the neighbourhood. Their views paralleled those of their parents. However, their appearances and behaviour were in striking contrast to their elders'. They acted and looked like American teenagers. They didn't seem much different from their more affluent counterparts, although their clothes were of cheaper quality and they had less of the costly paraphernalia typical of their age group. Unlike the richer kids, they were deeply patriotic. They may have looked like American teenagers, but they disliked America. They often went to McDonald's, but, as Vanja put it, "We go there because it is much cheaper now. It is even cheaper than Russian food and many pretty girls work there. And they have clean bathrooms."

One of his friends, a girl, said, "We always go there with the other girls to fix our makeup, and it's free."

But they think Americans have no respect for "the law" and "Americans think they are the biggest and the best and have no respect for anybody else."

"Americans think everybody wants to be like them, but it's not true. We don't and our friends don't. We just like the things they have."

Vanja said his parents and adults in general did not like America either. "We will show them yet," said Sasha. But when I pressed the point, they could not be more specific than to say, "Russia is going to be a superpower again very soon."

Sasha, the leader of the group, is known as a rocker. The boys attend various schools, some in three-year technical school programs, others in the local high school. Most of the girls go to high school, and most have boyfriends. They all love rock music and are very familiar with everything popular in the West, but they like Russian groups the most. Sasha plays guitar in a local garage band. They do not know much about the Soviet era, but they all "hate" the fact that Russia is no longer a superpower. They firmly believe it will "come back". Like their parents, they credit Putin for this and applaud him for it.

They differ in their views of military action and war. Surprisingly strong contrasting emotions were displayed when I asked about the war in Chechnya and Russia's actions in the Caucasus region. Like most Russians of all ages, they do not hold positive views of Chechens and harbour deep hostility towards them. They are not enthusiastic about the war, but most of the boys said they would go to fight there if they were called. "It is part of Russia, after all," said Yuri, "even though crazy religious fanatics stir things up there. We have a duty to protect the majority from them."

The attitudes were different regarding Russia's military involvement in Georgia or other former Soviet republics. They feel that it is okay for Russia to show America who is boss in the region, but they wouldn't be happy to fight against Georgians. "Georgians are cool people," said Sasha. "It's their American president who should be kicked out." When I asked for clarification, Sasha said it was on TV that he found out that Georgian President Mikheil Saakashvili was once a lawyer in New York City. (I checked later, and this statement turns out to be accurate.)

Vanja and his friends like to hang out in high-end shopping

malls which they reach by subway, but they dislike the rich kids they encounter there. There is a deep class resentment. They know nothing about the economic deprivations Russians suffered under Communism, and they do not know what "regulated economy" means, but they consider it "unfair" that some kids get to drive their parents' fancy cars, while they live in crowded two-room apartments with their parents and siblings, experiencing the shortage of money and daily hardships.

They take freedom of expression for granted and are not aware of any limitation on it. They are not aware of journalists who had lost their lives under mysterious circumstances while investigating "undesirable" subjects. They are not particularly interested in knowing about Soviet days and say they get irritated when their parents or teachers tried to enlighten them. But these teenagers feel intensely Russian. They all say that "Russia needs to be strong and respected again." (On the other hand, teenagers from affluent homes quite often said that they feel "global".) Vanja and his friends respect the Russian flag as a symbol, but do not care about demonstrations for or against anything. They attend gatherings of the Nashi youth movement when Russian rock groups play, as happens fairly often. They admire the fact that both Prime Minister Putin and President Medvedev have been spotted attending these concerts. But they also loved Schwarzenegger movies and Russian rap music, and they pointed out that Putin's martial arts skills prove that Russians have "their own hero" who is also a politician.

For Vanja and others, democracy is synonymous with law and order and a "good" political leader is one who can enforce them. They liked Putin because they believe he is "putting Russia in order." Their childhood memories of the 1990s—the Yeltsin years—is of chaos and crime, when their parents complained they were not getting paid their wages. "That wasn't democracy," said Sasha, and others nodded in agreement. All of them seem to have a great respect for law, but they were not sure what "the law" means. They ridicule the police and police corruption, although they consider it to be justified. "Cops have to take bribes, they don't make enough," was their view. They knew next to nothing about the Russian parliament, the Duma, and they do not care about it. When I asked whether they thought voting is important, they said, yes, it probably is, but they are not sure whether they would actually vote in any future election. But they did say that their parents, and especially their grandparents, vote.

I met with an older group, students at the prestigious Institute of Foreign Affairs of Moscow University. It is hard to get into and expensive, but is coveted by the best students. Through a friendly professor, I arranged to meet with a group of fifteen students. We started in a classroom, but the meeting continued informally afterwards. The students in this group represent the elite of Russian youth, the country's future leaders. I was keen to compare their views with the younger crowd. The students are in their early twenties, most of them living in Moscow under comfortable circumstances. Not surprisingly they are sophisticated and articulate. I was surprised to discover that their views are not essentially different from those of the younger group. The individuals in this group, however, all speak fluent English and other Western languages, and have daily contact with the world through their laptops and the Internet. They are familiar with the West's criticism of Putin's Russia, and they are ready to argue against it. They think Putin is perfectly suited to the job, because Russia will always need a strong leader, and that is how they perceive him.

"Democracy?" asks Masha. "Who says it has to be American-style democracy? We have our own, Russian-style democracy, and it suits us better. Corrupt state employees? It's inevitable during a transition. Eighteen years is a short time, and our economy is booming."

"Corruption will disappear," says Dimitri. "For now, it oils the system and serves a useful function."

Somebody says, "The economy is flourishing. The 1990s were a disaster. Now we have got it just right. Putin is rebuilding the strong centre of Russia and restoring Russia's place in the world."

Four of the participants of this discussion group were members of Nashi. In fact, they were among the leaders. One was Masha. She described anybody who is against the Russian status quo as a failure: "They cannot find themselves within the new order, and they blame the new system for their inability to make it." Nashi is organized in cells. There are cells which are responsible for organizing demonstrations and marches and cells responsible for membership. Those in the communications/publicity cells are responsible for making sure that the organization maintains the correct image. There is even a cell called "Our Army" and its job is to attract young men to enlist in the voluntary army. Masha is involved with the communications wing of Nashi. They meet, they talk, they demonstrate, and they have a sense of belonging.

Sergei is a part of an ideological cell, and is quite high up in the hierarchy of Nashi. He and other young men and women host discussion groups at his Institute. They organize debates about Russia's mission, identity, and political heritage.

I laughingly suggested that he sounded like a "Red commissar", but he took the suggestion seriously and essentially agreed with me. "Their role was immensely important," he said. "They were raising the consciousness of the masses, and so do we!" And then, perhaps not surprisingly, I heard some warm words about Lenin.

"Would you say you are a communist?" I asked.

"No," Sergei answered, very seriously. "We are not ready to put a label on ourselves, but we try to use the best from Russia's past and present, and invest it in Russia's future. We believe in participation, involvement."

I asked him how he envisioned his professional future after graduation from the Institute. He told me he sees himself working for the Ministry of Foreign Affairs. He wanted to be involved with Russian-Chinese relations.

"It's an incredibly important area of our foreign policy, and of our future in Asia."

Already fluent in English, Sergei studies Chinese. Putin is his absolute idol. He has even tried to emulate Putin's way of speaking and moving. Sergei met Putin in person at a small gathering of hand-picked national leaders of Nashi outside Moscow, and said that he will never forget the experience. Putin's appearance was unexpected, he just showed up. Of course it was carefully planned and prearranged but the participants were not told that. The element of surprise elevated the impact of the event.

Since 2005 Nashi has been organizing summer camps for young people, usually at picturesque spots by a lake or the sea, or in the mountains, often in the places where Soviet youth camps had been held. Subsidized Soviet youth camps were an inexpensive way for the majority of children and youth to spend summers in the countryside. At today's camps Nashi live in tents, with portable toilets and barbecues, and...Putin's portrait everywhere. They have political and ideological discussions, they sing songs and play music, and they unite in hostility toward the United States, the West, and specific geopolitical acts perceived as hostile to Russia. They always have a current enemy list. It includes members of the parliamentary opposition, Western politicians who have expressed harsh criticism of Russia, the oligarchs, and communists.

I predict Sergei will do very well in Putin's Russia. He is the kind of young man the Kremlin likes to invest in. It is significant that he comes from a more modest family background than the other students with whom I spoke. His father is a retired engineer and his mother is a librarian. They are not wealthy, and he is one of a few recipients of scholarships to the prestigious school he attends. He is rather disdainful toward some of his monied friends and he believes that most of the rich New Russians should be curtailed and taxed more heavily. "All these excessively rich New Russians are like a sick growth on the healthy body of my country," he declared. "It is plain and simple. The rich stole from Russia during Yeltsin's years. But justice will be done. They will have to pay it back eventually."

While it is not exactly clear what "they will pay" means, he is supportive of the Kremlin's moves against many of the Russian oligarchs. Oddly enough, most of my young interviewees, regardless of age, background, or education, were quite critical of extreme wealth, although they frequently appear to be in awe of it and its benefits. Some of them were wealthy themselves.

Nashi is not the only youth organization. Many exist under an umbrella called Other Russia and, more often than not, they also put Putin on a pedestal. They organize rallies against Communists, whom they despise. One of the groups, Moving Together, presents itself as a path to social and moral—and, some say, political—rectitude. Its leaders organize summer camps with the Russian Orthodox Church, and trips to historic cities. Its leaders state it has eighty thousand members—ranging in age from twelve to thirty—in sixty cities and towns across Russia. Members are expected to attend six concerts or plays a year, visit four historic cities, check out six books from the library, and volunteer at least once a month at an orphanage or senior citizens homes. Moving Together's leaders keep the focus on spiritual values and on Russian history and heritage. Members are expected to renounce drugs, alcohol, and foul language and to extol patriotism, healthy families, and similar values. Putin's lavish support and Moving Together's contacts high in his administration leads to speculation that it is a creature of the Kremlin, created to advance his policies. The leaders deny this, but they acknowledge that the organization receives money from local governments, including from Moscow's former Mayor Yury Luzhkov. In addition, corporations sponsor trips and other activities.

Moving Together occasionally targets Russian writers whom they consider immoral. Victor Erofeyev was the focus of their attacks for a while, and the author warned that the campaign posed a threat with its demand for strict adherence to prescribed values reminiscent of Soviet times. "Russia has lost its identity," he said, "and the search for this phantom is the most fashionable event in the country today. Everybody wants to find out what it means to be Russian, and these conservative patriotic groups exploit it." (Steven Lee Meyers, "Russian Group is Offering Values to Fill a Void," *New York Times,* February 16, 2003)

This was a theme in almost every conversation I had. Young people desperately want to believe in Russia, but the problem is they have nothing specific to take pride in. The Great Terror? Stalin? The rise of the oligarchs? The war in Chechnya?

There are paradoxes. Moving Together adulates Russia's past, and its present as personified by Putin. It uses structures and methods used by the Communist youth organizations, but they carry banners that protest against the Communist Party, and, in the same breath, against the exiled oligarch Boris Berezovsky. Berezovsky was a product of the wildest post-communist capitalist period of the 1990s, a power behind Yeltsin and a staunch critic of Putin. Everybody in Russia appears to agree that Russia has lost its identity. Everybody wants to find out what it means to be Russian, even if the quest leads to extraordinary juxtapositions of ideas and trends.

There is an entire new generation of young people who are not afraid and who are freer than any generation since the Bolshevik revolution of 1917. They display a remarkable ignorance about the depths of Soviet oppression and cruelty. When teens are told, for example, that the secret police limited typewriters to a handful of loyal Communist Party members, or that photocopying was illegal, they do not comprehend. They wonder if their computers would have been confiscated.

The Moscow teens I spoke with came from various social classes in the country's wealthiest region. Compared to any of them, the teens in the rest of the country are poor, but they share the same passion for Western goods: clothes, shoes, music, computers, and cellphones. All youth think of today's Russia as a democracy and they resent Western criticism of Russian ways. Law and order, something they associate with the Soviet era, are admired and are high on the list of what Russia needs. This is the primary reason that Putin is admired by young people from various economic groups, social classes, regions, and even organizations that do not appear to see eye-to-eye on other matters. All politically active youth, both those who see themselves as "democrats and liberals", open to the West, and the "ultra-nationalist" patriots who long to see a return to the strong Russia of Imperial or Soviet times and who reject Western ways, agree on the need for Russia to return to superpower status.

These observations were confirmed by a sociological study conducted in Russia, "Russia in 2010" which concluded that:

There is a "peaceful coexistence" of democratic and authoritarian orientations, of subjective factors in explaining political processes, and of moral grounds of power. The political consciousness of youth is extremely contradictory. An orientation toward Western patterns of politics and culture coexists with an extremely cautious attitude toward the West. A liberal emphasis on human rights coexists with a desire for the strong hand of authoritarianism. No significant differences between the political culture of boys and girls were found. We note, however, that girls are more socially oriented and pay more attention to culture as an important factor in the development of Russia. (Irina Milyukova, "The Political Future of Russia through the Eyes of Young Students," *Young*, vol. 10, 2002)

Under Soviet rule two national political youth organi-zations were empowered to educate, indoctrinate, and thus create citizens devoted to the totalitarian system: the Young Pioneers for school-age children, and Komsomol, the Young Communist League. Both were tightly structured and demanded a high degree of discipline and uniformity from their members. They provided ideological focus. The groups' activities were political, social, and cultural. One observes a similar structure and focus in Nashi and Moving Together. A new organization named Mishkii—Teddy Bears—is modelled on Young Pioneers and aims to instill patriotic values in seven- to fifteen-year-olds.

Another organization, called the Young Guard, is a pro-Kremlin direct action group for youth, similar to Nashi. It is the official youth wing of the ruling United Russia Party. Its name is taken from a World War II-era Komsomol underground organization in the Nazi-occupied city of Krasnodon. A very well-known book and film were made about it, entitled *The Young Guard (Molodaya Gvardiya)*. The film depicts heroic youths ready to be tortured and to die for their motherland. The organization adopted the name because of its symbolic significance. Unlike Nashi and Marching Together, the Young Guard has branches throughout Russia. It attracts many working young people. Early on it tended to be more militant and was always present at demonstrations. In recent years the authorities have less need for such demonstrations and, in fact, they actively discourage them. First it was Nashi members who stopped taking to the streets. Now the Young Guard is not called upon to take up public positions.

In place of militancy, authorities now call for more populist attitudes. Members of the Young Guard protested in Vladivostok against a city government that was slow to fix local highways. Another demonstration involved a protest against the use of Methadone in treating heroin addicts. In November 2008 the Young Guard held a demonstration supporting calls for Russia's borders to be closed to migrant workers in 2009 to provide more jobs for Russians during the global economic crisis. On one occasion the United Russia Party's Young Guard picketed the Federal Migration Service offices and the head offices of major corporations in Moscow, Nizhny Novgorod, Chelyabinsk, Novosibirsk, and Khabarovsk. The authorities claim that there is no link between them and such measures, because it would be impossible to close the country's borders to immigration. They also distanced themselves from a Young Guard proposal to have its members patrol the streets looking for illegal workers. Young Guard activities include military-style training, religion, music fan clubs, summer camps, and business programs for budding entrepreneurs.

All the youth organizations publish literature that speaks of restoring order, national power, and prestige to Russia, and all promote patriotism. Their T-shirts have such slogans as "Get High on Literature", "Help an Orphan", "Russia is Great", "Help Mother Russia", and "Leave Drugs, Get High on Russia".

Moving Together, in particular, claims to have enlisted many young people who had been on drugs or part of the street culture. When I spoke with members during a membership drive party on a Moscow street, they told me that belonging to Moving Together gave them not only a sense of belonging and a new identity, but also restored their sense of human dignity.

"When I took drugs, I thought I was Superman. When I was coming down I felt I was a worthless shit, but worst of all I felt desperately alone and without hope. Now I know I am Russian, part of a great nation with a mission and a future. I learn more every day. I help. I belong," said a young man who didn't give me his name. His sentiments were echoed by others nearby.

But not everyone agreed. A black-clad youth with a lip pierced said he felt that "No one who joins one of these groups can keep their individuality. They will swallow you, man." So I began to look for young Russians who did not ascribe to the ideology of joining and belonging that are dominant features of the youth movements.

Skinheads

SKINHEADS ARE EASY to spot everywhere in the world, but difficult to befriend. Their shaved heads, heavy black boots, and preference for black leather, metal chains, and tattoos set them apart. I spoke privately with an official of the Russian Ministry of the Interior who works in a department combating organized crime. He estimates that there may be fifteen thousand skinheads in Russia, with the largest number in Moscow—about three thousand. They have no organizational structure, and they gather in isolated groups of various sizes. Their key unifying factor is mutual recognition and support in public places and at gatherings where they act in unison even if they don't know each other, uniting against individuals and groups perceived as "others". The element of belonging is of major importance even though there are no governing rituals, though they are frequently referred to as neo-fascists. Most, including those on the fringes of the movement, are between seventeen and thirty years old, and the majority of the crimes they commit are racially motivated. My source from the Ministry suggested that some extremist politicians and the media supporting them exploit the skinheads to advance their own political agendas.

With considerable trepidation I once approached a group of skinheads hanging around a beer stand in a working-class neighbourhood of Moscow. My attempt to speak with them was not successful, perhaps because I am female. They generally scorn women and treat them badly. They recognized, with hostility, that I was a foreigner. "Go back where you came from," they said, spiking their words with unrepeatable language. "Russia is for Russians. You… " I got the message.

If my skin had been brown or black I might have been beaten or even killed. People from Africa and Asia have been murdered in unprovoked attacks.

Sometimes it is difficult to distinguish skinheads from neo-Nazis. Some skinheads belong to fringe right-wing nationalist groups, while others join in on the action if they see their peers with a similar style of dress and hair involved. But Nazis tend to know each other; they wear metal swastikas and black arm bands, and their activities tend to be organized.

In 2005 Russia declared November 4 as its National Day, replac- ing November festivities that had been celebrated under Soviet rule. The origins of the holiday are somewhat obscure; it celebrates the defeat of Polish invaders in 1612 and replaces a commemoration of the 1917 Bolshevik Revolution. For most Russians the day has no political or social significance; but in many Russian cities the neo-Nazis appear in force, marching with Nazi salutes and shouts of "Heil Hitler". The marches are unauthorized and disturbances are frequent, with police arresting the marchers. Other groups may show up as well, including Young Guards and people from the Marching Together movement. Their slogans echo the shouts of the neo-Nazis. "Russia for Russians," they shout. They scream hostile statements about illegal immigration. It is becoming a major issue in large cities, in part because many of the marchers carry clubs, knives, or even guns. Clashes occur when dark, foreign-looking people appear in the vicinity. The Moscow Human Rights Bureau reported a rise in xenophobic crimes in the first ten months of 2008, with 113 people killed and 340 wounded, a 50 per cent increase since 2007.

Goths, Emos, and Others

THERE ARE OTHER young people who affect a dramatically different look. I went to a club called Tochka (polka dot) to meet some of them. Their most distinctive characteristic is body piercings. They have metal in every imaginable place—nose and lips, ears and eyebrows, eyelids and necks, hands and feet, and any number of places that are barely covered. Girls favour black laddered tights and anything with black leather. Hair is dyed black, magenta, blue, or green. The goal is not to look attractive but to shock and to blend in with the group. Most of the kids who come to Tochka are in high school and they relate to teen subcultures, with music as the unifying factor, such genres as emo, hardcore punk, and goth. I found, though, that they focus almost exclusively on externals: clothes, piercings, hair, and rituals of behaviour. There is no ideological attachment or focus to their "rebellious" ways. The act of being different suffices. They clearly enjoy the discomfort it causes their elders, not unlike young people anywhere else in the world.

The key elements of these subcultures may become illegal in Russia. Moscow papers report that the government is working to outlaw them because they are perceived as a "dangerous trend". A paper entitled "Government Strategy in the Sphere of Spiritual and Ethical Education" proposed that the Duma enact legislation banning websites that cater to these subcultures. It proposes a prohibition on young people entering public buildings or attending school dressed in the attire of these subcultures.

Other proposals with the aim of "protecting children's morality" have been considered by the Russian parliament. Russian deputies, reflecting the attitudes of Russians in general, are not enchanted with Western holidays like Halloween which is considered quite offensive by many; it is considered to be disrespectful of the dead and "totally inappropriate to Russian values and culture". The toys, masks, costumes, rituals, skeletons, graves, and other paraphernalia provoke aggressively hostile reactions from Russians of all ages. The very young might be curious or frightened, the teens may consider them cool, if distasteful, but anybody older than that is repulsed by them. Death and related topics are not taken lightly in Russia. Other items on the agenda for parliamentary deliberations dealing with children's morality include items involving the serious issues of child pornography and youth alcoholism. Consideration has been given to introducing a ten p.m. curfew for all school-age children.

Subcultures such as emo, punk, and goth are often considered together with skinheads as things it would be better to eliminate because they endanger youth values and cause the young to question their place in society. Putin has consistently taken an interest in the upbringing of the younger generation and has often addressed the subject. In March 2005 he spoke to a session of the Culture and Arts Council devoted to the topic of children.

> I am going to speak of the problems that stand in the way of establishing a normal spiritual environment for the development of our young generation, an environment necessary to bring up a full-fledged, valuable generation of citizens. We have gotten rid of the domination of ideology in raising the young, yet we have not been able to replace it with approaches that are adequate to modern realities. Children's loneliness, their lack of supervision even in families, the devaluing of cultural values, and the deficit in upbringing—these factors are the basis of an increase in juvenile delinquency, drug addiction, and child neglect. We need new pedagogy, a new system of education in schools, families, and social institutions. To develop that pedagogy, we need to create a system of cultural values that conforms to today's reality.

Lengthy discussions on TV and radio and in the newspapers reflect his concern. Russia is no longer in the state of political, social, and economic chaos which dominated the 1990s, but the after-effects of the fall of Communism and the decade of transition linger. Excessive use of drugs and alcohol are tied to despair, crime, and suicide among the young. Promiscuity is linked to STDs and

AIDS. These problems supplant traditional spiritual values, respect for elders, and love for the motherland. Politicians, parents, teachers, and journalists are remarkably united in calling for broad government initiatives to counteract these trends and promote patriotism and national pride.

There is intense criticism of American movies and television shows that promote violence. Horror movies such as *Halloween* or *Friday the 13th* are a special target of scorn. In Soviet days there were government-subsidized "palaces of culture" where youth could get involved in activities ranging from sports to music and art. Now there is consumer culture, shopping malls, and the streets. Parents in a constant quest for revenue have less time than ever to devote to children and young teens. Movements like Nashi, Mishki and Moving Together are viewed as important alternatives to aimlessness, consumerism, and Western-style youth subcultures. There is a widely-held view that Russia cannot afford to lose the young generation amid the demographic crisis that is so much in evidence. This conviction justifies the ever-increasing politicization of these movements and organizations. Their critics, concerned that this mirrors Soviet-style indoctrination, are attacked by the supporters of these groups.

Alosha, the Counterfeit CD Seller

I ALWAYS RELY ON spontaneous interaction with people to get a sense of Russian moods and opinions and I try to engage people in conversation in markets, stores, cafés, buses, the metro, and on the street. My overtures are often rejected, viewed with suspicion or treated flippantly. But this approach has meant that I have been able to speak with a large number of young Russians spontaneously. A common denominator among the young people I spoke with is that none of them could remember the Soviet Union. Another is that I am a foreigner which, in their eyes, explained and justified my engaging people so much younger than myself in conversation. In recent years I have found people in public places more open to being approached than their counterparts in the 1990s.

All the young people I approached live in Moscow. They all speak English, some fluently. I insisted on speaking Russian with them and they appreciated it. At Gorbushka, a market for counterfeit electronic goods in Moscow, Alosha, a nineteen-year-old university dropout with long black hair, was selling pirated CDs. I observed him while looking at CDs and we began to talk about Swedish heavy metal, which is very popular among some teens. From there, I moved on to other topics. I asked him why he is no longer a student.

"The important thing now is money," he told me. "I wouldn't make half as much as a teacher as I make even now." He had studied education at Moscow University, both of his parents are high-school teachers and he had been a scholarship student. He has a younger sister, of fifteen still in high school.

"My parents bring home about $750 a month. That's about average, but it is not much." Alosha makes as much as $500 a month, sometimes more. He lives with his parents, but does not contribute to household expenses. However, he pays for the family's Internet connection and bought the PC that the entire family uses. He also pays for his sister's cellphone as well as his own.

"Those are the essentials," he said. "You cannot be without them."

Alosha does not belong to a group or movement, nor is he interested in politics. He said he does not know, or care, about the Soviet past. He dismissed Nashi, Young Guard, and Moving Together, although he respects people who belong, and he knows some who do. But he is more likely to hang out with a goth and heavy metal crowd. He thinks drugs should be legal and speaks of Holland as a great country because of its liberal approach to drugs. He firmly believes that "one has to rely on oneself and one's family. Family is the most important." He wants the world to respect Russia and approves of Putin because he thinks that "Putin takes Russia into the future and gains respect for Russia."

Alya, the Stripper for Putin

GUM, THE EXCLUSIVE SHOPPING mall on Red Square, is a jewel of art nouveau architecture. It once housed stores that were all but empty of merchandise, and it still had long lines. Today it is a beautiful place to buy expensive clothes. As I strolled through my attention was caught by a beautiful young woman sitting at a table in a small espresso café amid the elegant boutiques. She was examining a bad blister on her foot. She had taken off a very high-heeled sandal. Sensing an opportunity to strike up a conversation, I stop-ped and offered her a Band-Aid and sympathy. Both were gratefully accepted. Her name is Alya, and she works as a stripper. In a vulnerable moment, she was willing to converse with me without reservation. She had just broken up with Vitya, her boyfriend of six months. He had picked her up at 5 a.m. at the club where she works. They drove to his place, slept a bit, and then had yet another row. Alya said she'd had enough, left, and hobbled in her high-heeled working shoes to GUM. Since it was her day off, she had decided to treat herself to something nice. Her mistake was to have walked from his place instead of going back to her place to change into jeans and flat shoes. "But first of all, I need some coffee," she said.

Alya is twenty-two years old. In a city full of beautiful young women ready for anything, she is exceptionally attractive: blonde, tall, and glamorous. She was born in Moscow during Gorbachev's perestroika in 1985 and graduated from high school in 2003. Due to her looks she got a sales job at a fancy boutique in central Moscow, where she met the owner of the club where she was now working as a stripper. She didn't want me to know the name of the club, but in the course of our conversation it became clear that lap dancing is part of her job. She makes a lot of money, sometimes up to US$2,000 a week. She does not like to call herself a "stripper"; she uses the term "exotic dancer".

Her boyfriend is Armenian, but he has spent his entire life in Moscow and makes his living as a photographer taking nude pictures of exotic dancers like Alya for men's magazines, calendars, and cards. Her dream is to be featured one day in the Russian *Playboy* magazine. But she is worried: "I am getting older and there are many younger girls ready to do anything to get there." She broke up with her boyfriend because he wanted her to become an actress in pornographic films, and she didn't want to go that far. "There is constant pressure on girls to deliver more and more to club owners and patrons, and many do. What can you do?"

Alya has a dream of getting married, having two children and a house. She is saving money for her dream house, while living with a roommate in a rented two-room apartment far from the city centre. I expressed surprise at the apparent contradiction of a spread in *Playboy* versus a suburban vision. She said there is no contradiction at all. "Now we have choice. We have the opportunity to realize ourselves." She criticized prudish attitudes toward sex. She said she has had many boyfriends who have all thought that what she does for a living is "glamorous. They didn't mind at all." Her parents, however, pretend to not know what she does to earn money. They do not ask many questions, and she does not give them details. Everybody pretends she is a cocktail waitress and aspiring model. She has a younger sister, a "good girl" who is a high school student. Alya's mother is a post office clerk and her father, a maintenance technician for the subway system. They live in a two-room apartment in a typical, nondescript part of Moscow, a great distance from downtown.

I didn't expect her to know or care about politics, but I asked the question nevertheless. I started with the past: "Do you know much about life in the Soviet days?" She surprised me by telling me she knew a lot. Her seventy-something grandmother was retired and lived with her parents. Alya loved her "very much" and had heard a lot about old times from her. To my further surprise, she told me that her grandmother and her parents agree that "Putin is a great leader."

She has a vague, romanticized notion of the Soviet reality with her grandmother as the source of information. Her parents think that life is better now although they both work hard and are always worried that they might get sick or lose their jobs. Her grandmother has often told her about "the beautiful life in the Soviet Union". She told her about the carefree summer camps she attended as a girl and about activities in the Palaces of Youth, and "patriotic parades and gatherings." Alya is not exactly sure what the parades and assemblies were all about, but she thinks that "those were the days when one believed in something other than money." She said she would like her children to "believe in something". Her mother was forty-five, "worn out and over the hill". Her father drinks.

"Why do you think Putin is such a great leader?" I asked.

"Because he makes the world respect Russia and he will make Russia a great country again." She thinks he is comparable to one of the great tsars and that "he is after the very rich, who stole from Russia."

I was struck by her obvious hostility toward the glitter and "the beautiful people" surrounding us at GUM. She both envies them and wants the things they can apparently afford, but at the same time I observed an undiluted class rage against the rich that would have made Karl Marx proud.

Young *Businessmeny*

VLADIMIR POTANIN is a Russian oligarch, chair of one of the largest conglomerates, Interros. He made his money during the privatization drive of the 1990s, during which well-connected individuals could buy state-owned assets for a fraction of their real value. The process was shady, and the billions that they made are considered questionable, so most of the oligarchs have invested heavily in cleaning up their images. Like many others, Potanin steers clear of politics. He wants to be in the Kremlin's good graces and to conduct business in a transparent, although profitable, fashion. He wants to be seen as one who gives back to society, so he created a foundation which provides scholarships to young Russians who want to study leadership in business. Every year, 1,330 of the best students from across Russia are awarded a stipend. They can study abroad, even in the United States or Canada. The winners are called

"Potaninites" and receive US$50 a month. They take part in workshops based on real-life business situations, and they receive assistance in finding employment.

I met one such student, Natasha Markova. She had been twenty-one and a student at Moscow University majoring in economics when she got her award in 2005. She was very political and, at the same time, she rejected any form of politics. She does not belong to any party or organization, and is critical of the current leadership, although this is not a criticism of the growing authoritarianism of the Kremlin. She believes that "authorities"—that is, the state—should control more rather than less. "Business needs security and a safe climate," she said.

She speaks very good English and had spent six months taking business courses at New York University. She said she had learned a lot, but found American society too permissive. "I never felt at home there, and I don't think American capitalism would work well in Russia."

She is, nevertheless, quite critical of many aspects of doing business in Russia, including unfair business practices, extortion rackets, and interference from bureaucrats for personal gain. She believes that stricter regulations and controls could effectively deal with these problems. She works in a commercial bank, where she is advancing "very nicely". She has made lots many friends through Potanin Foundation workshops and maintains lively contact with many of them. Some have opened their own businesses, such as shops, restaurants, and service outlets. Others work for banks or large companies.

She sees herself and her peers as pioneers in starting mid-size businesses in Russia. She is enthusiastic about Potanin's contribution to her good fortune, but embarrassed to dwell on the mechanics of the early privatizations which led to his and other oligarchs' fortunes. "Russia needs a middle class and millionaires, not billionaires," she said. But she was upset when I mentioned the fate of another oligarch, Khodorkovsky, who amassed a fortune with the oil giant Yukos only to be imprisoned for alleged tax evasion and relieved of his holdings by the state.

"It will be our generation that will change things," she told me, "and it is up to us to see that we are responsible in business and that we are, in turn, treated fairly and responsibly."

The *businessmeny* are a new phenomenon in Russia. They have a sound economic and business education, they speak fluent English and other languages, they are familiar with the West first-hand, and many are assuming important positions in Russian and international companies. Others are developing their own small businesses, or dream of doing so with the conviction that their dream can become reality.

And Who Do You Blame?

THERE ARE OTHER young people in Russia besides political youth, unconventional youth, and young *businessmeny*. In 2004, the Russian Health Protection Ministry stated that three million young Russians were addicted to drugs: the number of registered addicts between ages thirteen and twenty-five is higher than this. Ten years ago Russian youth knew about heroin, cocaine, and hashish by hearsay. As of 2009, more than 80 per cent have experimented with various drugs. The Ministry estimated that without a concerted effort to stem the tide, Russia would soon have ten million addicts, who would pose a serious threat to the nation. Millions of people, young and old, are alcoholics.

The recent Levada poll found that 20 per cent of Russia's young people were "dissatisfied with life". A further 20 per cent said that their material situation was "very bad" and there is no hope of improvement. One common denominator unifies people under forty, regardless of their success or failure in life. The young feel that one's prosperity depends on oneself alone, while the middle-aged and elderly believe that "the prosperity of citizens depends largely on the country's leadership." But the young are not always ready to expend the effort required: many of them drink, take drugs, or do not work hard, and they feel lost in the new Russia. They tend to be apolitical, with attitudes expressed in statements like "It has nothing to do with me" or "Who cares?" They generally do not vote or attend demonstrations, nor are they involved in group activities. But even among these people the perception is that "Putin likes sports, behaves normally, has an answer for everything, and is respected abroad."

The Beliefs and Values of Youth

A STUDY BY THE Levada Centre investigated how the young Russian *businessmeny* differ from people who grew up in the Soviet period. The main difference is the absence of fear. In essence, today's young people do not have a past; they know very little about it, and they do not want to. The director of the Centre, Professor Yuri Levada, states:

> They are free from old fears and old interests alike. The young people don't have to destroy or negate anything, because they have no past. The country buried its past in 1991 and we do not have the continuity of generations that is common in industrialized countries. Any economic and social changes proceed almost unnoticed and very gradually in stable foreign societies. They have their traditions, customs, and socially accepted rules. But we moved from an abyss to a precipice in the past decade. And this greatly influenced the development of inner values and behaviour of the rising generation.

The Levada study also stated that the absence of fear can coincide with absence of respect for the law. Therefore, young people consider it normal to cheat on taxes or in other aspects of business and personal life. There is plenty of cynicism and a lack of compassion. However, on the positive side, people were are well-informed and they relate easily to foreigners, significant because, in the Soviet past, contacts with foreigners were sometimes forbidden and subject to punishment. Outsiders had always been treated with suspicion by the authorities, in particular the secret services. The young tend to be optimistic about their earning potential, and they fully expect to enjoy the good life. While most of them shun politics, they support the current political climate and leadership.

Another study (Alexei N. Bolshakov, "The Next Generation's Thinking on American Business's Future with Russia") adds some interesting insights. A look at the age distribution of respondents provides an unexpected finding. It is often said that Russian youth is the most pro-American segment of Russian society. However, even though eighteen- to thirty-five-year-olds were slightly more pro-American than other age groups, the deviation is almost insignificant. Further, while appearances may suggest that Russian young people look and sound like North Americans their age, they do not see eye-to-eye on many issues. For example, young Russians uniformly supported their leader's stand on the war in Iraq; they were opposed to it and against American policy. American approval ratings of their president—Bush was still in office—varied by age group, were lowest among young people, and were generally low for all groups. Russian youth support Putin overwhelmingly, more than any other age group.

A 2003 study by the Harvard University Institute of Politics ("Campus Kids: the New Swing Voters") found that more American students were Democrats than Republicans but that the gap was closing. Most students did not perceive themselves as partisan. Russian surveys have likewise found that most youth were not loyal to a particular party, but they strongly support Putin's United Russia Party. Only seven per cent of the young supported the Communist Party, compared to 33 per cent of those over fifty.

The Economist surveyed young people and, like the Harvard study, found that young Americans were far less liberal than their baby boomer parents on sex, drugs, and abortion. They tend to lean to the left on social issues and to the right on economic policy. Russian youth were found to have similar conservative views. Two-thirds of Russian youth declared some kind of religious affiliation, while one-third declared themselves atheist. Even more unexpected, although I had observed it, was that most of those professing to be religious do not attend church. Older Russians professed similar convictions.

A survey carried out in Russia in 2003 by the Russian Public Opinion Research Center concluded that 73 per cent of Russians believe in God and angels. Half believe in life after death and in heaven, but only about half of this group believe in the reality of hell and the devil. Forty-four per cent of Russians believe in miracles. Twenty-five per cent believed in ghosts. (These statistics may shed light on Russians' aversion to Halloween. Russian parents support media criticism of Western Halloween customs, and Russian youth generally do not consider it to be fun or camp.)

In a 2004 study the Russian Centre of Sociology found that the young generation did not trust any of the country's institutions, except the Church and Putin. Only half trusted Russian democracy and fewer than that had any faith in institutions such as the Duma, political parties, or the military. They explained their faith in Putin with their perception that his character and personality reflect integrity and vision. Any notions that are associated with him are popular with them. During the 1990s, by contrast, only three per cent of young people trusted Boris Yeltsin.

Sociologists have suggested that the faith that the young have in Putin is a reflection of their parents' and grandparents' attitudes. Russia may be witnessing a levelling, with various age groups tending to share opinions. Sociologists have also suggested that the moral values of Russia's generations have essentially evened out.

In the 1990s I often observed that family conflicts were common, but after the turn of the millennium they declined. The young and their elders appear to be different on the surface, but they watch the same TV channels, are exposed to the same advertising, shop at the same stores, and have similar responses to the same political reality.

The studies found considerable idealism combined with conservatism among all generations, expressed by the trust in the head of state and the Church. But like the young, the older generations tended to not practice their Christianity.

The Centre of Sociology at Moscow's University of Sociopolitical Research studied more than two thousand people between the ages of fifteen and twenty-nine in 2004 and again in 2007.

After the year 2000, their increased faith in Russia's stability, in the possibility of making money, and in Russia's international standing were all associated with Putin and his office. Although many young people refused to participate in politics, they were willing to entrust their future to the "strong leader". They applauded free market entrepreneurialism while accepting that society was becoming less open.

ROMIR, Russia's largest marketing and research institute, conducted a national survey on Russian attitudes to mass media. Seventy-six per cent of all Russians agreed that there should be censorship of mass media. Younger people were less supportive of this, and women of all ages were more in favour than men.

Pravda in 2002 reported that women of all ages also supported banning Barbie dolls from Russian toy stores. Barbie was only one of many items that people believe should be banned because of the "harmful effects they have on young children", according to the Ministry of Education, but the doll was singled out by Putin. Her "outrageous curves" do not promote "wholesome values" in young children. The Education Ministry stated that Barbie in particular "awakens sexual impulses in the minds of the very young" and "encourages consumerism among Russian children." The Ministry sent a request to the Duma to create a commission to examine the psychological effects of toys and games which could provoke aggression, fear, and "premature sexual manifestations". A Ministry document stated: "The Russian market is overwhelmed with various toys of foreign production, some of them damaging and not appropriate for small children."

Such a move would be seen as an attempt by the Kremlin to control the identity of young Russians. Putin is keen to foster ideals of family and patriotism, along with a belief in the potential of Russia to be a great power. When I travelled in Russia in 2008 Barbie was still on the market and the media were debating her influence on Russian girls. Psychologists were expressing concern that the Barbie doll could upset the normal development of girls by imposing the Western norm of a slim figure at an early age. "The doll fosters a particular ideal of body shape. Young children aim to correspond and dream of growing up to be two metres tall with slim hips and huge breasts." Recommendations to the manufacturer to offer various body types fell on deaf ears. Barbie continues to sell, market forces being at times stronger than ideological considerations, even when backed by Putin.

The official rejection of Barbie and the degree of popular support it engendered was a somewhat light-hearted example of the massive changes shaping popular perceptions of America. There are new interpretations of American "values and images". Popular magazines describe American society as obsessed with work, career, making money, and personal success. These values are not admired. Commentators discuss how these values leave no room for compassion, love, and the need to share—and that they have created a society of unfeeling, intolerant people obsessed with money, possessions, status, and achievement, leading to eventual "degeneration of culture and humanity". Russia and particularly Russian youth are warned against such values. Russian media ridicule popular aspects of American life such as its obsession with weight and dieting, the money spent on pets, politically correct thinking, and even the concept of sexual harassment, which most Russians apparently find ridiculous.

It has been difficult to assess to what extent these interpretations of America have a responsive audience, but without a doubt there is a difference in perception between people aged thirty to fifty and those under thirty. For older generations, America still personifies the West. The young tend to see America as "lacking culture", "primitive", and no longer "worthy" of emulating.

Leisure Activities

RUSSIA HAS ALWAYS been a nation of readers, and theatre is a national passion. Russians point to their love of literature and poetry when they talk about the Russian soul and their differences from others. This was true in both Imperial and Soviet days and applied to people with every level of education. These passions were cultivated in private and public lives and successfully used during the Communist era to influence and politicize people.

Free-market capitalism is changing the cultural picture. Twelve per cent of respondents to the Levada study said that they hardly ever read fiction; 25 per cent read newspapers at most once a month. The following example illustrates the dramatic change: 60 per cent of the Levada respondents (who were between eighteen and twenty-nine) never go to theatre or classical concerts. It is a widely held belief that the majority of young people spend their free time in disco clubs or cafés, but this is not quite true. Only a third of teenagers and older young people regularly visit them. Half of Levada's respondents never do. Twenty per cent participate in sports, while a good number mentioned that they like computers.

Role Models in the Movies

THE YOUNG IN RUSSIA like going to the cinema, and American movies are the most popular. Until roughly 2006, 75 per cent of all movie-goers were under thirty, and the majority were teenagers. It wasn't simply the choice of movies. In Soviet days, American movies were rarely shown; then after the fall of communism, hardly anything else was shown. The same pattern was true for films shown on television, but while those shown at the cinemas are new, the ones on TV were old. Action and combat movies were, and remain, most popular. Fans enjoy qualities like physical strength and aggressiveness as well as exotic scenery, fast action, and special effects. But in recent years over forty per cent of the population choose not to go to movies because they have been repelled by these qualities. They prefer content and a social message that stresses intellect, the prevalence of justice, social good, and other ideals.

The young are attracted by the types of heroes in popular Western movies: often single young men—cheerful, optimistic, handsome, with a sense of humour, enterprising and inventive about getting out of difficult situations, strong, often aggressive, and successful in the end. The heroes don't talk much and are successful with women. They may or may not be on the side of law, but they have hearts of gold.

Some evolution has been observed, though in some popular television shows there is a new practice of America-bashing, with action movies and their heroes as the target. They are ridiculed as examples of American arrogance and self-absorption, and the main characters are one-dimensional and simplistic. The very qualities that first attracted the films' audiences are being put down as too primitive for Russian viewers, who, after all, have "Russian souls".

The few Russian movies that were made in the 1990s and later are quite different: either poor copies of American action films or dark movies depicting bleak and desperate post-Communist reality. The heroes are doomed by fate and circumstances. They were often defeated, or they perished, but the films were not popular with youth. Since about 2005 there has been a change as filmmakers are no longer left on their own to find financial backing; there are subsidies from the Ministry of Culture for the creation of wide-screen historical epics celebrating the Russian past. The films are popular with all age groups, especially movies set during the 1917-1921 civil war that followed the Bolshevik Revolution. A new spirit and new heroes are emerging, that evokes patriotism and nationalism as part of the officially sponsored search for the new Russian identity.

The Return of the Russian Soul

THE SEARCH FOR IDENTITY coincides with a phenomenon I first observed in the 1990s that has become more persistent, although it has assumed different characteristics. During conversations with young Russians during the 1990s I was struck by their insistence that Russians are different from people in the West and that "Russia cannot be Russia without the Russian soul." David Manicom, in his excellent book *Progeny of Ghosts* (Oolichan Books, 1998), wrote:

Soul is the word the theoretically atheist Soviet-Russians prefer; the Russian soul, Ruskaya dusha. This mysterious entity—real enough, I believe, however hard to character-ize—had also produced Tolstoy, Shostakovitch, Akhma-tova, Pasternak, Sakharov, and had revered each and every one of them.

For there to be a future for Russia there had to be a revival of spiritual values, which meant a revival of the past. Manicom writes, "Russians are obsessed with the making of memorials to keep the ghosts of history alive." The belief is that Americanization and commercialization represent the greatest threats to the Russian soul. Much was said about Russia and its people being conditioned for hundreds of years to become a people who "prefer to be ruled and taken care of by the state" and who want their leaders to be "like tsars". For many, Communism seemed to be a continuation of what they already knew, and the Putin era is familiar and welcome.

In *Looking West? Cultural Globalization and Russian Youth Cultures* (Hilary Anne Pilkington with Elena Omel'chenko, Moya Flynn, Elena Starkova, and Ul'iana Bliudina, Penn State University Press, 2002), the authors describe the impact of globalization on Russian youth culture after the collapse of Communism, when Western media and products entered the emerging Russian market in full force. They found that while young Russians embrace and consume a variety of Western products, they remain critical of Western values and keep them separate from Russian culture. They developed selective attitudes toward things Western. The authors conclude that "Russia's response to globalization continues to throw up challenges to Western hegemony because its under-standing of 'self' and 'local' defies the rules of the globalization process." It was found, for example, that while Russian youth listen passionately to Western music, they consider Russian popular music to be superior because they perceive it as "music for the soul". The lyrics and the philosophical dimensions are important to them. What is popular in Russia music was not techno or rave but a soulful rock, full of poetry and meaning. The poetic element links the generations, because for centuries poetry has expressed the Russian "soul". Pilkington and her collaborators found that while young people look west, they do not consume "the West". Globalization has an impact, but it has not led to the abandonment of Russian values.

The new movies reinforce this sense of Russian-ness so that in the last few years Russian movies have begun to counterbalance the impact of American cinema.

Accepting the Russian perceptions of "negative" values supposedly representing the West or America, and comparing them with the "positive" Russian values yields a number of juxtapositions: Western rationalism versus Russian emotionalism, Western selfishness versus Russian generosity, Western individualism versus Russian collectivism, Western superficiality versus Russian genuineness, Western materialism versus Russian spirituality, Western hypocrisy versus Russian sincerity, and Western coldness versus Russian warmth.

Russian Youth and Democracy

THE POLITICAL SYSTEM in Russia has been undergoing transformation for two decades. The development of citizens takes place in an environment of political and non-political conditioning elements including family, peer group, school, the arts, and mass media. These elements channel basic personal orientations toward authority, conflict, order, violence, tolerance, freedom, and discipline.

Under communism there was a single, rigid, dogmatic value system. While historically collectivism was the rule, today a greater diversity of views is the norm, though collectivism is still perceived as morally superior to individualism. The re-socialization is of enormous scope with a new political vocabulary and new political standards which have emerged and had to be assimilated. Despite these upheavals most of the young people who I met, and those studied by the authors mentioned above, consider "big politics" boring. Their knowledge is abstract. But the younger they are, the more they tend to associate success with the ability to subordinate themselves to the system.

The young understand politics as a state governed by laws. The Yeltsin regime was considered weak and undemocratic. The Putin government represents, in their eyes, an improvement in strength and democratic character. Civic responsibility and participation in the affairs of state rank low on the list of democratic values that the young embrace. But the lack of interest in politics is coupled with a desire to become an elected politician, in a trend towards political opportunism. My respondents tend to think it is acceptable for a minority to rule a majority. They have no problem with social inequalities, saying that they obey the law, without having a clear understanding of it. They do not wish to understand how political authority operates and their emotional perception of politics is that they feel sympathy for institutions such as parliament, but they are not to be trusted.

Family, Friends, Life Companions, and Sex

MY PRIMARY INTEREST is sociopolitical, but I am often surprised at how readily young people would discuss a range of other topics. I reviewed my tapes and notes and selected twelve topics that arose in almost every conversation. The topics emerged from questions I always tried to insert: What do you think is the most important thing in life? What matters most?

The phrasing of their responses varied, but most of my respondents stated that good friends, family, and life companions mattered most. Some examples:

"Well, I think that my friends are really important for me, but my brother and I are very close, so he is more like a friend because we see each other every day. But I have kept friends from childhood, since I was about ten years old."

"My friends are like, basically, my life. I spend a lot of time with them. It seems like I can do anything with them, say anything to them. And they're special to me. Considering that when I leave my house and no one understands me, I get frustrated. I see my friends and I can tell them stuff like what happened to me."

I commented that it sounded like their friends were more important than the family.

A seventeen-year-old emo youth said, "My family is important to me, to support me, help me out, and harass me. I mean, they made me the way I am now. They don't believe that, and my mother refuses to believe that I'm like this now because of her. I'm wearing clothes like this because of them, maybe to antagonize them. My friends are my other part, more my emotional part. Whereas my family are the ones who always give me a hard time, but, in the end, I know they love me." (Emo youth followed a stream of music that emerged from hardcore punk.)

Another said, "My father and I fight constantly. My brother and my parents don't see eye-to-eye either. My brother is another story altogether. But he is ten years older than me. It also depends on the friends you had. He had a bunch of skinhead friends and we are not close. But my friends are more my family than my family is."

"Well, with family you feel obligated to love and respect them because you don't get to choose them, but you're stuck with them. But friends you choose. So if I choose these people to be my friends obviously I'm going to love and respect them because it's my choice. But family, I have a brother and a sister. My brother and I never used to get along. Now we do. My sister and I are on and off. It's like it goes through spells, stages. So I get along with them. I don't speak to my father, but I get along with my mother and my grandmother. My grandmother has always lived with us and helped raise us. But it's like my parents don't understand me, but I don't understand my parents either. I don't know what they think about certain things, or why they are the way they are. So I think it works both ways."

"My friends—I have very distinct groups of friends. There are drinking and fighting buddies, there's not a whole lot of intellectual thinking going on. They just go out to have a good time. Booze and whatever. Then there's the rest of my friends, those I can talk to or hang out with. It's two totally separate groups. People don't understand. I don't want the two groups to ever mix. I want them to stay separate. I'm not going to say that I have a split personality, or maybe it is a bit, but when I go to work, I turn a switch in my head and it's a totally different mentality. I interact with them differently than I interact with these friends. And it's because of that that I get along with each group, but I'm sure that the groups would not get along."

"As far as my friends are concerned, I used to be a loner. I was always a year younger than people in the same grade. Now I think I depend too much on my friends because I have many friends, more than I even care to keep in contact with sometimes, which is unfortunate because some are very good friends of mine and I don't maintain contact with them. Sometimes I prioritize and some friends just don't make the cut. I depend on them too much because if they don't meet with my expectations I get very let down by this. I have very good friends but only a few of them, and the rest is just a huge body of, like, casual friends. Earlier this year there was a period where I was not speaking to one of my best friends, for half a year. Well, it hurt me tremendously, but the thing is that I depended on that person so much that it was a tremendous void for me when that person was gone, and I think that my friends have become too important and I try to deemphasize them if I can."

I asked an emo boy "What about your parents? Do you feel there is a generation gap and you cannot communicate?"

"Yes. Basically when my family sees me they think I am a freak. They see me, my whole family, my parents, my relatives, they kind of see me as an object to make fun of, and with my friends it's not like that.

"I clash with the rest of the family and they always make fun of my hair, always make comments. It's kind of like I'm the different one. That's the way I always see it. My uncle makes fun of me all the time. So do my aunt, my mother, my father.

"The power of my mother is the power of the hand of God. She has absolute control over me. She gives me all the freedom I need, but if it comes to a point where she wants me to do something, then it will be done and I won't like it. So much guilt. My whole family is run on guilt. Everything I do is out of guilt. That's the way I see it. Everything I do is from guilt. The older I get, the more power they try to get over me. Last night I came home at, like, a quarter to two, like, big deal, here we go again."

"I'm a girl, and in my house there is a huge double standard. I consider myself to be very strong, pretty smart, maybe a little bit too loud-mouthed and I'll get in trouble, but I think that my parents are afraid because I'm a girl. There is another problem too. My older brother does absolutely nothing wrong. He's like perfect."

"With women, parents are worried, they are afraid, they are concerned. I was an immaculate conception I think. I've never heard the word 'sex' mentioned in the house. Don't talk about it, it doesn't exist, nobody ever does that."

"Friends are probably more important than your parents," someone said.

"No!"

"They are!"

"They're close but they change."

"Friends you choose, family you are stuck with. Well, that's not a nice thing to say, but…"

"I guess some friends really aren't your friends. They backstab you."

"They betray you."

"But do you think that friends are becoming more important in people's lives these days than in the past?" I asked.

The response was a collective "Yes!"

"Do you think friendships between men and women are possible?"

"Yes. It is the best friendship."

"I've been best friends with a girl since grade two We speak every night, but have never had any physical contact, sexually."

"But say that you have a girlfriend or boyfriend. How do they tolerate friendships with the other sex?" I asked.

"They either deal with it or leave it because my friends were here before you came, and they'll be here when you're gone."

"But, you know, that's very different from our parents' generation because they had real taboos on having friendships with persons of the opposite sex. Once you got married you had friends, but you would never have women friends for the husband and male friends for the wife. So that's also a very big change. I think that's what I'm observing."

"What about marriage?" I asked.

"Marriage is not the most important thing. It's important to have somebody you love. The marriage is not the big part."

On this subject there was a major difference of opinion between the genders. Virtually all the females I talked with, individually or in groups, felt that marriage was the logical conclusion of a good relationship. They did not seem to be against living together with a boyfriend for a while if they could manage it financially. And this attitude was new because only ten or fifteen years ago, girls I spoke with would tell me that marriage was a required progression from living together. They would not even contemplate the one without the other. That is one of the biggest dif-ferences between women under thirty I spoke with in the 1990s and the young women I've met more recently.

"If you have the financial security and a job, I think that's when you marry. And when you're going to have children."

"I would get married for kids. It's a big thing." .

"What about sex?"

"It is for both men and women. So it doesn't really matter if a man or a woman sleeps around just for fun. It doesn't make me think any less of that man or woman. They are equal. But being really involved with somebody is preferable to just sleeping around for fun."

"I don't agree. Women are different from men."

""Yes, they are!"

"They are better."

"What do you mean, better?"

"Women are more spiritual. Men are more animalistic."

"Does that create a difficulty in terms of the relationship between the sexes?"

"Yes. Even though a man and a woman speak to each other, they may not understand what each other means."

"But is it society that makes us different, or psychology?"

"No, it's physiology. Men cannot have babies. That's why women are better. They are future mothers."

"I wonder if there will ever be a time in the future that there won't be any difference between men and women?"

"No way, impossible. Never."

"No, I don't think so."

"So there will always be these communication barriers because of the differences?"

"Yes, yes. But it's not always a barrier because we complement each other. When we work with girls you see things from a different angle, you can combine the best of each. And it's a woman's job to make us better than ourselves. It's easier for them."

"Well, these differences are probably what causes the attraction, right?"

There was never a sexual revolution in Russia or the Soviet Union. Unacknowledged and blatant sexism was common. Russians felt left behind in this sphere. At times it felt like they tried to overcompensate by going to extremes. They declared things which seemed to be in direct contrast to what one was observing. Russia was always hypocritical in its attitudes toward sex and toward females as sexual beings.

Tatyana in Alexander Pushkin's novel *Eugene Onegin*, published in final form in 1837, defines the model for Russian womanhood. She placed dignity, loyalty, and duty above love, particularly physical love. She personifies conventional morality, in which woman's role is to elevate the man. He might be driven by sexual force, but she is supposed to be above it, ennobling him in the process.

Also from the nineteenth century, the novels of Fyodor Dostoyevsky feature wicked women as well as prostitutes with hearts of gold. The works of Leo Tolstoy have "sinners of the flesh" who are ultimately punished for their sins. Sexuality is, for both sexes, the domain of men. For women it represents suffering and doom. In Russia there was always a double standard and hypocrisy in all matters concerning sex. A brief encounter with "free love" after the Bolshevik Revolution lasted only a few years and ended in hardship for millions of women who had to raise fatherless children. It was followed by a return to "traditional family values" and unfounded claims of equality between the sexes in all spheres of life. In the new millennium the double standard persists even though the under-thirties professed a total rejection of it. While the young sound different from their older brothers and sisters, the depth of the rejection is questionable.

Only ten years ago Russian women twenty and under were telling me that they "would become helping and nurturing wives and mothers" to their achieving husbands and future children. When I saw them on more recent visits I found childless divorced women or single mothers, bitter and angry and struggling to make ends meet. These were the young women who had rejected the values of their Soviet-era mothers and their professional accomplishments. They were avid readers of *Cosmopolitan* magazine and they absorbed TV commercials promising that beauty and youthfulness would give them everlasting happiness. The bought these "truths" and now they are paying for them.

The twenty year-old women I met recently are more seasoned, knowledgeable, and cynical. They know that youth and beauty don't last, and they know that investing in a relationship cannot be their only capital. They are rediscovering the value of education, as their mothers and grandmothers did, but with a new twist. Possibly it is part of the new Russian identity being created, but Tatyana was back in vogue. The new Russian woman was to be the special carrier of a new spirituality. She might live with her boyfriend, but she sacrifices to his "animal nature", ennobling him in the process. For her, long-term family values are the most important. New myths are being created. The mass media promote the notion that Russian girls are "softer, more feminine, gentler, more modest" and more interested in family values than Western girls. They are "the hope of a new spiritual Russia".

I heard that "Everybody will eventually marry and have a family, but it is a woman's job to keep up the moral standards and instill them in the children." "You marry if you love somebody, and then you work on it." It is always the woman who will "work on it."

When asked "Do you see your marriage and family life as similar to your parents'?", Typical answers would be: "My parents are divorced. So is my sister." "But divorce is not, like, the end of the world. It is bad, but it can happen." "Divorce is more and more common in Russia. I don't know why." "I think young people are more worried about the future than our parents were." "The most important thing is to find somebody you can love and trust. And then you marry and work on it."

Good Health

MOST OF THE PEOPLE I talked with mentioned good health as being one of the most important things in life. But an estimated three million Russians were undermining their health as a result of drug addiction. More than this number of Russians between thirteen and twenty-five are drug addicts registered in a drug rehabilitation program. Where ten years ago average young Russians knew about heroin and cocaine, now 80 per cent have at least tried hashish, marijuana or something stronger. The Russian Health Protection Ministry predicted in 2000 that there would soon be ten million hard-drug addicts. In post-Communist Russia the average life expectancy for men has dropped from sixty-three to fifty-seven. Russians have begun to realize that they are contracting AIDS in growing numbers, changing the perception that it is a disease of homo-sexuals and people of African origin.

Concern for good health does not seem to impact on the young people's experimentation with drugs, nor with their excessive smoking, drinking and unsafe sex practices. The people involved with youth organizations have a much keener awareness of these issues. Some have been active in combating them both within and outside the groups. Needless to say, heavy drinking and smoking were and still are part of most Russians' lifestyle. Ironically, they are rarely mentioned when good health issues are being considered.

Good Education and Success at Work

THE THIRD MOST IMPORTANT issue for young people was especially apparent when I spoke with students at the elite Institute of International Relations. Unlike in Soviet days, education is no longer free. The more prestigious the institution of learning, the more expensive it is. There are scholarships, but for the most part higher education now depends on the ability to pay. The post-secondary institutions in Moscow and St. Petersburg are the most coveted, and the most expensive. Parents pay because in Russia students don't work while they study. This is a tradition from Soviet days. Also, the curriculum is demanding and really does not permit combining the demands of study with paid work. The children of wealthy parents are assured of access to higher education; less wealthy students compete fiercely for a limited number of openings with scholarships attached. These students generally have paid tutors who help them prepare for entrance exams that are necessary for scholarships. But access to higher education for poorer students who do not receive scholarships is almost impossible. Some privileged teens travel to study abroad; favourite destinations are British and American universities.

Knowledge of English and computer skills are required across the board. The educational path and professional prospects of a young person are also determined by the social and economic standing of their parents, their place of origin, and only then, by their talents and abilities. From the outset there are hierarchies. The young I met are becoming more aware of the facts about their advantages and restrictions.

There is one other way to advance in the realization of one's academic and professional potential, and that is through the youth organizations like Nashi, the Young Guard, and Moving Together which provide financial assistance to their members.

Wealth and Money

ABOUT HALF THE PEOPLE I interviewed listed money and/or wealth as the most important thing in life. But this has a variety of meanings. Most of the young in Russia today, both country- and city-dwellers, from wealthy or poor families, are exposed to visions of wealth in the media. The exposure is constant and relentless. In the big cities there is the added element of luxuries for sale at many stores. Visual contact with affluence was absent during their parents' and grandparents' younger lives. Their problem was scarcity of goods. For the young today, it is the abundance. There is a continuous pressure to acquire and buy, and, in most cases, an inability to do so. Although many of the young I spoke with denounced American-style consumerism, they nevertheless yearn to consume. This desire creates a drive to succeed that makes them study harder and compete more, but it also lead to stress and despair. In Soviet days, their parents could blame the system if they didn't get what they wanted. Their children are more likely to see themselves as failures or failures-in-the-making if they don't do as well as others.

Masha, a high school student, said:

> When my mother was a child, everyone had the same clothes and the same shoes. Now we have all different styles. But that just means it's harder for us, because somebody always has to have something better and more expensive. And when we are funky, other kids laugh at the brave kids who wear new and different styles.

University students tend to be less preoccupied with clothes, cosmetics, computer games, sex, and drugs. They have their sights set on their future prospects and dream of high-paying, prestigious jobs, fancy apartments, and fast cars. They are too young to remember the daily hardship of the Communist era or the climate of protest and alienation in which their parents grew up.

Friends, family, and companions; good health; a good education and a good job, and, finally, money and wealth are what the young consider to be the most important things in life. Some include freedom of choice further down on their list of priorities. Some add good relations with people and the respect of people. A few said they want to "feel needed". Surprisingly few talk about having children as the most important thing in life, despite a fixation on family values and on the role of the mother. A few said they want to "live interesting lives", without being specific as to what that might entail.

The New Leaders

AFTER THE CHAOS of the 1990s came the law and order of the Putin era, along with growing centralization of power. Western observers insist that democracy is being eroded, while the majority of Russians applaud the changes that have come under Putin.

It has been frequently assumed in the West that the young, who did not grow up under communism or in its shadow, would be open and enthusiastic toward Western-style democracy. This does not appear to be the case. (Nadia Diuk, "Russian Democracy in Eclipse: the Next Generation", in *Journal of Democracy* 15/3, 2004)

The Levada Centre has reported that a quarter of all voters are young, and that in the 2004 election, most of young people supported Putin's United Russia Party. Even those who are not politically involved approve of the direction in which Russia is going. These young people are well informed, computer literate, know English, and have more money than their parents ever dreamed of having. In the 1990s young people dreamt of leaving Russia. My more recent respondents feel good about living in

Russia and think of going abroad only for pleasure as tourists. They are living better and their level of satisfaction is higher than in previous generations. They are enthusiastic about free enterprise, but they also welcome state ownership of natural resources and key industries and, in general, they expect the state to play a paternalistic role. They are upset if this is absent, particularly in the areas of health care and education. They are in agreement with their parents and grandparents in these expectations.

In the 2004 Levada study the young indicated that their trust in the office of president is high, with an 81 per cent approval rating. They expressed a marked preference for a strong leader. In terms of trust, only friends and relatives rank higher at 91 per cent. Sixty-six per cent trust the Russian media, which the West considers is influenced by censorship and untrustworthy. Political parties rank low in trust, with 78 per cent not trusting them, although the people vote in great numbers for Putin's party. They expressed a low degree of support for the military with draft-dodging being popular. They were increasingly nationalistic and their level of tolerance for people from the former Soviet republics was decreasing. Prevailing attitudes among the young demonstrated racism and hostility toward Africans and Asians.

The repercussions from the 2008-2009 world-wide economic downturn will probably have an impact on the attitudes of Russia's young people. Threats to their ascent into the middle class may increase their support for a centralized, paternalistic state and a strong leader. Their nationalism may evolve further into xenophobia.

PART FOUR

Russia's New Identity

Vladimir Putin.

Putin's Russia

IN MY YEARLY TRAVELS in Russia during the Yeltsin era, the mood swung from wild enthusiasm at the beginning of the 1990s to deep despair later in the decade. By contrast, the mood during the first decade of the new millennium has been one of continuously growing optimism. When I asked people, young and old, what they think Russia is becoming and where it is going, the responses were in striking contrast to the previous decade. Essentially they feel Russia "is coming back up" and they are optimistic about its prospects.

The twentieth century saw the collapse of two Russian empires. Democratic rhetoric, the turn to the free market, along with the expectations and promises—all ended in collective disappointment, with hardship for some and, for most, unprecedented corruption and institutional chaos. The country was in disarray: the economy was in a shambles, there was a leadership vacuum, the military was disintegrating, people had no jobs and no income. Russia was fast becoming a pathetic, laughable giant, falling gracelessly on its face. Russians saw this and resentment grew towards outsiders, primarily the United States and Western Europe.

There was barely any applause when little-known Vladimir Putin became president in 2000. He was re-elected four years later, an undisputed leader with massive popularity. After two terms in office his popularity exceeded that of any other world leader. Almost everyone expected that he would be elected again and again, once a proposed constitutional amendment that would permit him to serve an extended term was passed.

In 2007 *Time* magazine named him Person of the Year and labelled him the "Tsar of the New Russia". It might have been more accurate to have named him Person of the Last Eight Years, because he brought Russia back to its former status as a world leader through a consistent, determined, and uncompromising process that brought him support at home and mixed reactions abroad.

When he became president Russia was on the brink of collapse. As he said, it was "ravaged by inflation, devaluation, default, and by terrorists and outside forces that openly incited separatists in order to weaken Russia. State power was ineffective, with much of the economy in the hands of oligarchs or openly criminal organizations, and Russian media outlets often acting in the interests of particular corporate groups." (February 8, 2008 speech to the meeting of the Advisory State Council)

It is significant that Putin's assessment of the 1990s did not differ markedly from that of Western commentators. But while he described his vision as Russia's future as progress, Western observers wondered whether if it was not already resulting in a return to autocratic repression. However, Putin does not profess to be a democrat in the Western sense of the term. Freedom of expression is not a primary objective for him. He wants stability above all, and the population appears to back him on this.

New President?

ONE EVENING in early March 2008 two youthful, slender, leather-clad men strolled across Red Square from the Kremlin to a light-flooded outdoor stage. The thousands of people gathered there applauded. It was the day of a presidential election, and there was a rock concert in the evening. The men weren't rock stars, but Putin and Medvedev, the president and president-elect.

One could not help but compare the scene with that of thirty or forty years ago, when Brezhnev and company were elected.

First Deputy Prime Minister Dmitry Medvedev was Putin's chosen successor as president. Medvedev had spent one day campaigning. He taped a ten-minute address to the nation that was broadcast repeatedly on national television—as news. He said that the country needed "political stability" and pledged to ensure "the reliable protection of Russia's sovereignty and to protect citizens' freedoms." And that was that! Despite complaints from the other political parties that Medvedev had been given illegal advantages in election coverage by the state media, despite attempted public marches of dissent and charges that his election was "shameful" and "illegitimate", it was documented that he received 70 per cent of the vote, with 67 per cent of the electorate casting a vote. Western governments declared their willingness to work with him, although some officials declared that "the people of Russia are going back to the days...where they don't have the right of free election or a free society." Russian analyst Aleksei Makarkin posted on the Internet that "Medvedev's success shows that the majority of the electorate has legitimized the vote of the single solitary voter, Vladimir Putin."

Why Putin and What Is His Secret?

IN AN ARTICLE ENTITLED "In Putin, the Populace Sees What It Wants to See", Olga Kryshtanovskaya, head of the department for the Study of Elites of the Institute of Sociology in the Russian Academy of Sciences, analyzed the reasons for Putin's enormous popularity. She posed the question: what had he done to deserve such popularity, trust, and forgiveness for any act he might wish to commit? She looked at his admirers and critics. A survey conducted by her institute provided an answer.

Most respondents found Putin to be "normal", a "normal" president in an "abnormal country" after ten years of "abnormal politics". His supporters were many, and diverse. He was loved and admired by state officials, ordinary hard-working people, housewives, young and old alike. They viewed him as a hard-working, unassuming man who, above all, loves his country. They were impressed by his honesty, decency, and incorruptibility. Putin is dramatically different from Yeltsin, or any other Russian leader. He is fit and muscular, holds a black belt in judo, and his carefully cultivated image of masculine strength has been translated into an image of having the ability to restore Russia's greatness. The all-girl Russian band Singing Together echoes his appeal to females with their lyrics, "I want a man full of strength/who doesn't drink/

who doesn't hurt me/who won't run away. I want a man like Putin."

He is disliked by oligarchs and by some in the military and security services. Contrary to opinion in the West, where pundits delight in labelling him a "former KGB spy" and in presenting Russia as a state run by a newer version of the KGB, Kryshtan-ovskaya observed that Russian security service personnel have found that their expectation of having a major say in Russian politics had not been met. Their initial euphoria gave way to skepticism and then a bitter feeling of having been deceived. In 1999-2000, many officers, after long vacillation, switched their allegiance from the Communists to the new president. The recent trend is in the opposite direction.

Throughout the 1990s the West, in a simplistic fashion, attempted to see Russians as either democrats or Communists. As it has turned out, there are few of either left. Another simplistic but more accurate portrayal of Russia might be those who are with Putin, and the few who are against him. Is he, then, a Communist or a democrat? Does he adhere to any ideology? And what is the Russian identity, at the end of the first decade of the new millennium?

In Search of a New Identity

PUTIN IS OFTEN DESCRIBED as lacking in any ideology. Communists charge that he is a democrat, but democrats feel that he is a communist in hiding. Western media routinely refer to him as an autocrat and a KGB man at heart and in politics. Possibly the secret of his success is his ability to appear to be all things to all people. But I do not ascribe to this notion, and believe that he is working hard to create a new Russian identity infused with elements of both Soviet and Imperial Russian ideologies. I think he is doing it with skill and determination, but that it is not an easy task. Robert Parsons of Radio Free Europe has noted that "the idea of defining a concept of Russian nationalism is almost as old as Russia itself—and just as elusive." If the current global economic crisis does not result in a major economic downturn in

Russia, and if the process of economic improvement continues there, Russia's "new" identity will be solidified. As *Moscow News* reported in August 2008:

> The resurrection of Russia's financial system from a bankrupt pariah to an integral part of world finance has been perhaps the most extraordinary recovery story in global finance of the last ten years. Tremendous value has been created.

The only group which has felt the crunch thus far have been the very, very rich oligarchs. The so-called ordinary people do not feel the anxiety that is being experienced by almost everyone in the West. If this situation can be maintained, trust in the official rhetoric will be further reinforced, and the process of shaping the new Russian identity will proceed.

Let's Start with Lenin

WHEN I ASKED SOME of the high school students I met what they knew about Lenin, they were somewhat bewildered and amused by the question. I had seen some old Communists on television celebrating the eightieth anniversary of Lenin's death, and I made a reference to the small crowd I had seen on Red Square. I didn't expect hilarity as a reaction.

"He was this funny looking short guy with a cap who they still keep in the mausoleum," said one.

"He was a good man who was a leader of the revolution," said another.

"He wanted all people to be equal," they all agreed.

"He was very popular."

"If these old guys still remember him he must have done lots of good."

There were vague reminiscences of grandparents' remarks and stories, but the overall sense of Lenin's contribution to Russian history was that he "gave the power to the people, and that was good."

Another high school student added, "Lenin was like Putin, because Putin also represents the people."

The university students were somewhat more sophisticated in their views. One said, "Lenin started what Stalin concluded." Another said, "Lenin should be held responsible for crimes against humanity."

While some of the students knew about labour camps and purges, they were not clear about when they had occurred and whether Lenin or Stalin had instituted them. Without exception, they were ignorant of the number of victims and heard my suggestion that there were tens of millions of them with considerable skepticism. But most of the young people I spoke with believe that Lenin's mummified remains should be removed from the mausoleum on Red Square where they have rested for nearly eight decades. Older Russians felt as strongly that his body should be preserved "indefinitely, as it looks now, for another hundred years or longer." It has to be pointed out that Lenin himself didn't wish to be preserved. It was done against his will by Stalin's command. Putin has remained detached and supports neither opinion.

In the West any discussion of Lenin's ideological legacy and Stalin's application of it, deformed or not, always includes a condemnation of their regimes, covering the period between 1917 to1953. There is always an emphasis on the repression and the human cost. What is rarely mentioned is the monumental tempo of economic and social development that was achieved during this period. The West also generally ignores or minimizes ideological advances that took place as a majority of Soviet citizens were followers of Lenin and Stalin and believed in the promise of Communism. Most older Russians still consider the mausoleum on Red Square to be a "holy" place. It is a symbol that still carries a great value for people who spent their whole lives as Soviet citizens. It is not unusual to hear younger people talk with pride about the time the Soviet Union became a superpower and "everybody respected us." Some commentators believe that these emerging positive views of Lenin echo Soviet propaganda.

Stalin and Other Heroes

EVERY SUCCESSFUL NATION has heroes. The Web World Public Opinion polling group conducted a poll on "Who will lead the world?" One question had to do with national heroes. Predictably, the British voted for Winston Churchill, Americans selected Ronald Reagan, South Africans endorsed Nelson Mandela, and Germans picked Konrad Adenauer. The Russian state television channel Rossia conducted a similar poll, asking Internet users to choose, from a list of five hundred, the twelve names that best symbolize Russia. To the consternation of the sponsors, the mostly young respondents placed Stalin at the top. The young respondents had never experienced anything remotely resembling Stalinism, so, for them, Stalin represented the era when Russia was strong, feared, and respected. And, judging by the number of positive and always enthusiastic books about him in Russian bookstores, it is apparent that he once again inspires curiosity and admiration. Moral considerations aside, this choice presents a dilemma. Russia's political stance is generally anti-Communist. Can they reject Stalin as a hero when he was the choice of most of those responding to the poll?

There is another conflict in the making. When Communists in St. Petersburg officially requested that the Orthodox Church canonize Stalin, the Church rejected the idea as a monstrosity. The Russian Church has risen to an unprecedented height in post-communist Russia. Contradictions multiply. Alexander Solzhenitsyn, the Nobel prizewinner who immortalized Stalin's millions of victims and whose legacy the Kremlin was trying to co-opt in 2009, was also selected as a Russian hero. Can both Stalin and Solzhenitsyn be venerated? To resolve this ideological conflict, the TV station explained that the choice of Stalin was the work of hackers and a provocation. The results were nullified. For a while, to the joy of monarchists, Tsar Nicholas II was ahead, but then the situation began to change.

Suddenly, a new name appeared as number one. It was Alexander Nevsky, a medieval statesman and military leader. He is a symbol of Russian nationalism and of defiance toward the West. But Nevsky was, as well, a major role model for Stalin. The new list included not only Nevsky, but also Alexander Pushkin, Fyodor Dostoyevsky, Tsar Peter the Great, Vladimir Lenin, Empress Catherine the Great, Tsar Ivan the Terrible (also a role model for Stalin), and Stalin, this time number twelve rather than number one. The odd thing was that Nicholas II, the last tsar, who was executed by Bolsheviks on Lenin's orders and who was generally perceived as a weak leader, disappeared from the list altogether. And while Lenin occupied fifth place, numbers six and seven were tsars who were known for their authoritarian rule, military victories, and territorial expansionism. The final ranking of the twelve heroes was to be determined after an hour-long presentation on each one.

God Is with Us

THE ORTHODOX RELIGION was introduced to Russia in the tenth century when Prince Vladimir Sviatoslavich of Kiev adopted the Byzantine version of Christianity with the objective of creating a common religious identity for the people under his rule. Over a thousand years later, in today's Russia, Russian Orthodoxy plays an increasingly important role. Russia's vast territory is the home to more than one hundred ethnic groups. Most are Russian, and for most of the second millennium religion played the role of the unifier. It is not an accident that recurrent motifs in Russian poetry are the vastness of the land and the might of the people. Vastness and might have always been emphasized by rulers and the Church alike in fostering Russian nationalism. There was always enormous pride in the vastness of her territory. Russia considered itself the Third Rome after Rome itself and Constantinople, the original seat of Orthodoxy. Since the beginning of the eighteenth century there has been an ambivalence as to whether the "real" Russia belongs to the East or the West. Peter the Great (reigned 1682-1725) "opened the window to the West," bringing Russia into the

European sphere. But the francophile Russian upper classes were in for a cruel awakening when Napoleon invaded Russia in 1812. After that, European identity began to take second place to a Russian identity. The "ordinary people", the Russian Orthodox Church, and Asian connections were back in favour. A division had formed; Russians began to see themselves as *Zapadniki* (Westerners) or Slavophiles. The great artistic and literary accomplishments of the nineteenth century that made Russia famous throughout the world reflect this ideological duality. The Russian Orthodox Church, although always subordinate to the Tsars, played a major role in glorifying Russia and Russian-ness. Nineteenth-century literature, religion, and art produced the concept of the "Russian soul", creating the image of a special spiritual dimension that the Russian people were believed to have and this contributed enormously to Russian national identity.

After the 1917 revolution the Church lost its land and holdings and the formal separation of church and state was decreed. To implement the decree, a liquidation committee was created to evict the monks from their monasteries, many of which were then destroyed or vandalized. Liturgical vessels and church bells were melted down. Reliquaries were defiled and broken open. Religion was declared to be the opiate of the masses and it was virtually banned. Dramatic change began in the 1980s during Gorbachev's perestroika (reconstruction). The millennium of Christianity in Russia in 1988 was celebrated on a grand scale. That year, nearly two thousand new Orthodox religious communities were registered in the country. In 1990 a collection of freedom of religion laws was passed. Many restrictions were removed from religious communities. At present there are over five thousand Russian Orthodox religious communities. Church buildings and monasteries were returned to the Church and were often renovated, and new ones were built. Moscow's famous Cathedral of Christ the Saviour, demolished in 1931, was rebuilt as Patriarch Alexis II declared its rebirth as "a sublime act of piety and penitence".

Alexis II died at the end of 2008 at age 79. His funeral took place at the Cathedral that he and President Boris Yeltsin had helped rebuild during the 1990s. Public events and entertainment broadcasts were cancelled by order of President Dmitry Medvedev, reflecting the elevation of the faith to the status of de facto state religion under Putin. Medvedev had earlier described Alexis as a "genuine spiritual leader" and "great citizen of Russia". His successor, Kirill I, was enthroned in January 2009. He is known to be a strong opponent of the West and an advocate of religion's presence in every sphere of Russian life, including education. Political analyst Andrei Piontkovsky, who holds posts at the Washington-based Hudson Institute and the Russian Academy of Sciences, stated that Kirill might turn out to be "even more active in anti-Western campaigning and emphasizing that Russia is a different civilization, and that the West is hostile to Russia," adding that "The Church has returned to its position as the ideological department of the ruling party. It has nothing to do with Christianity."

From the time of Gorbachev and Yeltsin, no public or state event can occur without the Church's formal blessing, sanction, and presence. Virtually every state institution has a patron saint. As the newspaper *Vokrug Novostei* reported,

The tax police are under the heavenly protection of St. Matthew, who, before he went on to write one of the gospels, had been a tax collector. The navy is under the protection of the apostle Andrew; the paratroops are watched over by the prophet Elijah. The troops of the Interior Ministry are protected by the sainted Grand Prince Vladimir, while the infantry is shielded by St. George. The Corps of Engineers has the Holy Prince Daniel of Moscow, and the border guards are protected by a folk hero, Ilya Muromets, who is the only legendary character to have been canonized by the Orthodox Church. The strategic wing of the air force is protected by the sainted military commander Fyodor Ushakov, while the strategic rocket forces are watched over by St. Varvara.

In *Slate* and *Vanity Fair*, Christopher Hitchens reported that Fidel Castro published a syndicated column entitled "The Russian Orthodox Church", in which he called it a "spiritual force". He elaborated on "the major role the Church played at critical times in the history of Russia." He received the Church's envoy and suggested building a Cathedral of the Russian Orthodox Church in Havana, a monument to Cuban-Russian friendship. The combination of the return of close ties between Cuba and Russia and the new importance of religion and the Church in Russia is no accident. It signifies a new course in Russian policy and a new ingredient in Russian identity.

Mighty Russia

THE CONCEPT OF A STRONG Russia is not new. It was always part of the collective self-image in Imperial Russia and the Soviet Union. Even at the beginning of the twentieth century, when the Russian Empire was often referred to as a "giant on legs of clay", Russians thought of their Great Mother Russia as an immutable, immove-able idea. Its vindication is Russia's most striking feature: its land mass. Since its founding, it has been one of the largest countries in the world, occupying about one-sixth of the land mass of the entire planet. It is about twice the size of the United States or China, and larger than Europe, Australia, or South America. Its mostly flat vastness stretches across half the planet. It has great rivers and lakes and extreme climatic contrasts. It is immensely rich in natural resources. Russians are known to say, "Russia is such a rich country! Everybody is still stealing from Russia and yet there is much more to steal!" It has virtually every mineral and is the most self-sufficient of industrialized countries, and a major exporter of commodities upon which other countries are dependent. As well, it is a country of extremes, having known great poverty, cruelty, abuse of power, and loss of life. On the other hand, it has accomplished much, although any assessment of those accomplishments varies depending on one's ideological orientation.

The 1990s, after the Soviet Union disintegrated and Russia was undergoing the transition to a free market and democracy, riddled as it was with contradictions, tribulations, and failures, was a major blow to Russia's collective ego. The sense of loss, defeat, and humiliation unified Russians of all ages and backgrounds. It did not matter whether one was a Communist, a reformer, a nationalist, or an internationalist. All Russians felt that their country had become a second-rate superpower that no longer mattered, which set the stage for Putin.

It has always been part of the Russian political tradition for foreign policy to be left up to the leaders. These issues rarely inspire the people. Even as the world was applauding Gorbachev's disarmament initiatives during the 1980s, many Russians barely noticed. Some were critical because they believed that he was weakening the country. Yeltsin's lack of foreign policy angered people. The economic and social problems of his regime intensified Russia's sense of not having a leader; crucial for a nation that has traditionally longed for a *vozd*, a strong leader. From tsarist times Russians have understood that they were led to strength, might, and respect by their leaders. When a leader was weak, Russia would fall on hard times. Such was the case with Nicholas II, the last tsar.

From the day he assumed power, Putin set in motion a propaganda machine, making use of the formidable techniques developed during the Soviet era which successfully reinforced in most Russians a nationalistic longing for a great Russia. It emphaized real and invented intrigues by the West which had brought Russia to her knees.

Visions of the New Russia, combining the glorious elements of the past, began to appear in the media. Money became available for movies with themes from the past. It was a technique employed by Stalin's propaganda apparatus, when famous movies like Sergei Eisenstein's *Ivan the Terrible* and *Alexander Nevsky* were created. They served as role models for Stalin and fanned the flames of Russian nationalism and collective pride in Russia's past.

With stability restored, with people getting paid their wages and the laws curtailing the mafia, there was a new faith that "Russia is coming back." Kryshtanovskaya said the main reason for the stability is that even the poor saw a chance to be better off. In the 1990s, she wrote that "one segment got richer while the rest got poorer. Today everybody is getting richer, and everybody is busy earning and spending money." She also pointed out that there was probably no other point in the country's history where more wealth was being generated. During the economic expansion of the 1960s and 1970s, much of the wealth was eaten up by the military-industrial complex. "Today a lot goes into welfare, and that is probably unique."

Restoring Russia to greatness is central to Putin's vision: the country will be a great military power, its military-industrial complex will be revived. National resources are to be reclaimed. Corruption and economic crime are to be controlled and eliminated. Perhaps for the first time in the country's history, Russians are aware of foreign policy and international developments. Western criticism reached a peak during the brief 2008 Georgian war. Russian public opinion was firmly behind their country's action. The perception that Russia is a born-again superpower has been growing. There is a sense of pride that Russia was asserting itself and standing up for its own interests because having a decisive voice in the former Soviet republics is considered vital. Increasing visibility of the United States in the region is considered a threat to Russia's security. NATO's expansion eastward is a direct provocation, so any action to counter these moves is applauded by a majority of Russians.

The newfound confidence would not exist were it not for Russia's re-emerging economic power. As some economic analysts note, the resurrection of the financial system from the status of a bankrupt pariah to an integral part of the world financial system has been perhaps the most extraordinary recovery story in global finance in the past decade. Alexander Pertsovsky, CEO of Renaissance Capital, has said, "The demand for what Russia has to offer, from natural resources to technology, will therefore only grow, placing Russia in a fantastic position to play its historic and geographic role as the link between East and West."

Putin re-nationalized oil and gas and then mining. He negotiated to have the foreign debt slashed, freeing Russia of international obligations and allowing it to trade with whomever it wishes. He introduced policies independent of the West and he entered into economic partnerships with Indonesia and China. Europe's dependence on Russian energy resources remains Russia's key economic weapon, and it is being used skillfully.

Many analysts think Russia will be able to maintain its edge during the global economic downturn, just as the Soviet Union weathered the Great Depression. That stability remains in the collective memory and Putin's vision draws on it. Most Russians believe that the Soviet regime had concrete goals and plans for the country's development. They are enthusiastic that Putin's new Russian identity will restore these valuable aspects of the past. Kryshtanovskaya said that Russia's ambition is to create a bipolar world in where it will act as a global counterbalance to the United States. The timing of the South Ossetian conflict, she thinks, was carefully planned. "The leader of the first world, America, is in a particularly disadvantageous position because of the economic crisis and the upcoming change in leadership," she wrote prior to the 2008 American election. "Russia, by contrast, is on the rise. It has economic growth, oil prices are high. Global circumstances are such that they allow Russia to hope that it will be regarded, as in the past, as the leader of the second world, even if the borders of this second world are vague."

She believes Russia's ambition is to create a mini-Soviet Union that would group Belarus, South Ossetia, Abkhazia, and perhaps eventually Transdniester, Moldova's pro-Moscow rebel province. This new union, she says, would be open to all countries that oppose the United States, including Iran and Venezuela. But she stresses that "This doesn't mean we are isolationists, that we are Stalin's Soviet Union. We remain open to contact with the West, not as a pupil, not as a younger brother, but as an equal partner." This sentiment is echoed by virtually all Russians, young and old, rich and poor. It is stronger than any differences.

Véhicule Press

www.vehiculepress.com